Praise fo
A Perception of a Difference

This book validated my own approach to life and work. It shows the importance of commitment, discipline and ambition. *Sales people that are in outside sales, i.e., insurance, real estate, anyone in one-on-one selling away from a home base office setting should read this book. It is great for new people to have as guide, **how to!** to refer to when their desire to make the next contact diminishes.*

—Retired car dealer/store owner

"This book is steeped with the genuine wisdom that comes from walking a mile in those size 10 shoes. There are no glossy quick fixes and instant gratification miracles. The principles shared by Wes stand the test of time, helping sales people to build very firm foundations under their chosen careers. I loved the 'Dad's Sayings.' This apple didn't fall too far from the tree."

—Germaine Cabe, Real estate and business brokerage

"The book is highly valuable to me even in my profession. I realize now that I am in a competitive business and will use the book as a reference in running and growing it. The marketing chapters were very useful. It was a new concept for me. I very much enjoyed the book due to its anecdotal stories mixed in amongst learning objectives. Though I am not in a typical "sales" position, I found all aspects of the book not only interesting but also valuable in running my practice. It is impossible to gain all the value from this book in one reading."

—Dr. Alan Gaveck, Podiatric Physician and Surgeon

Three weeks after writing my original comments I find myself reading sections of the book again. The story about giving fifty families work for five months is very compelling to me, and the story about the motorcycle company is very useful. Last week I copied and used chapter 12 in a sales meeting with all of our employees. Its message was perfect for us and everyone liked the chapter.

—Mortgage Broker

"It [the book] represents a solid practical approach to the entire process. Short examples provide a light-hearted meaningful way to make a point of the principles being emphasized. Easy to relate to and understand."

—Banker and banking consultant

I particularly enjoyed the last chapter. Right on the money! Reading the book made me feel nostalgic for an earlier, slower time when sales people treated customers like people rather than "the quick sale," and took time to really get to know their needs. Thank you for the opportunity to preview your book.

—Teacher

The Stories Are True

Except for certain members of my family and a few people who appear several times because they made a great difference in my life, all names have been changed to protect the privacy of the individuals who shared these stories with me or were involved in them with me.* All the stories are related in the first person though the majority happened to someone else and were related to me. I have used this approach to better pass on to you, the wisdom contained in them. You will learn this wisdom as you read and relate them to happenings in your life, not by preaching from me. Some of the stories will make you laugh; some will bring tears to your eyes; many are unforgettable.

Enjoy!

Wesley W. Zimmerman

---

*Please see Acknowledgements at the end of this volume.

We waited in the lobby to meet a surgeon who specializes in knee repair and replacement. We were there on the recommendation of another specialist we like and trust, who repaired my wife's shoulder. We were at ease and looking forward to learning how Amy's pain might be eliminated. The door opened.

"Amy, you're next."

When the door closed behind us, this person introduced herself. She was the surgeon, not an assistant. As she shook my hand, an overwhelming negative feeling filled me. Her hand felt like a dead fish does when you lift it out of a cold lake. At the end of a 20-minute examination and discussion, we walked to the car.

"That person is never going to work on my knee!"

"I agree. When did you make that decision?"

"By the time we reached the examining room… I felt I was just another project to her, not someone she could care about."

We were making a buying decision. The knee specialist was selling. Our trusted shoulder specialist was marketing the services of this knee specialist. The sale was lost because of a negative perception of a difference that formed in our minds without our conscious knowledge or control. That is the power of *The Perception Of A Difference (POD)*.

In this book you learn how these perceptions work in every buying decision and how you use them in Marketing, Selling, and Customer Care.

It will be a fun, fascinating, and very useful experience.

Wesley W. Zimmerman

THE
PERCEPTION
OF A
DIFFERENCE
ONE

The Power in
Buying,
Marketing,
Selling,
Customer Care

The Business Enhancement Team
Scottsdale, Arizona

Table Of Contents

> *The Power Of The Perception Of A Difference (POD) makes your*
> *dreams come true and enables you to make a difference by making the*
> *dreams of others come true.*

> *When you understand the process of buying you possess a tool that*
> *can improve your life and the lives of others. This is especially true*
> *when your work involves Marketing and Selling.*

> *Any job in Marketing is a great responsibility because Marketing's*
> *function and responsibilities in a business are widely misunderstood.*
> *This misunderstanding is often one of the causes of the problems that*
> *result in low sales and management disagreements.*

> *The easiest way to see the breadth as well as the gross detail*
> *of Marketing in a company is by seeing an example. This one*
> *is a beauty.*

Now that you know what Marketing really does, it is time to discuss what many people think is the only thing it does.

Selling takes over in the buying process when interactive dialog with a human is necessary for you to complete the buying decision. It is the realm of the professional salesperson. This chapter is designed to give you an overall understanding of the sales profession. The emphasis is on the practical and what actually works. You will find it useful if you are considering a career in sales, are selling currently, or are responsible for a sales operation.

Selling is an educational process which the professional salesperson executes effortlessly every day. These stories help you do it well and reveal the rich rewards of this lifetime effort.

In the process of asking questions, you generate new ideas in your and the customer's mind. This moves you up the four levels of sales professional without your realizing it's happening. As you read these stories compare them to your recent experiences and discover how much you've grown.

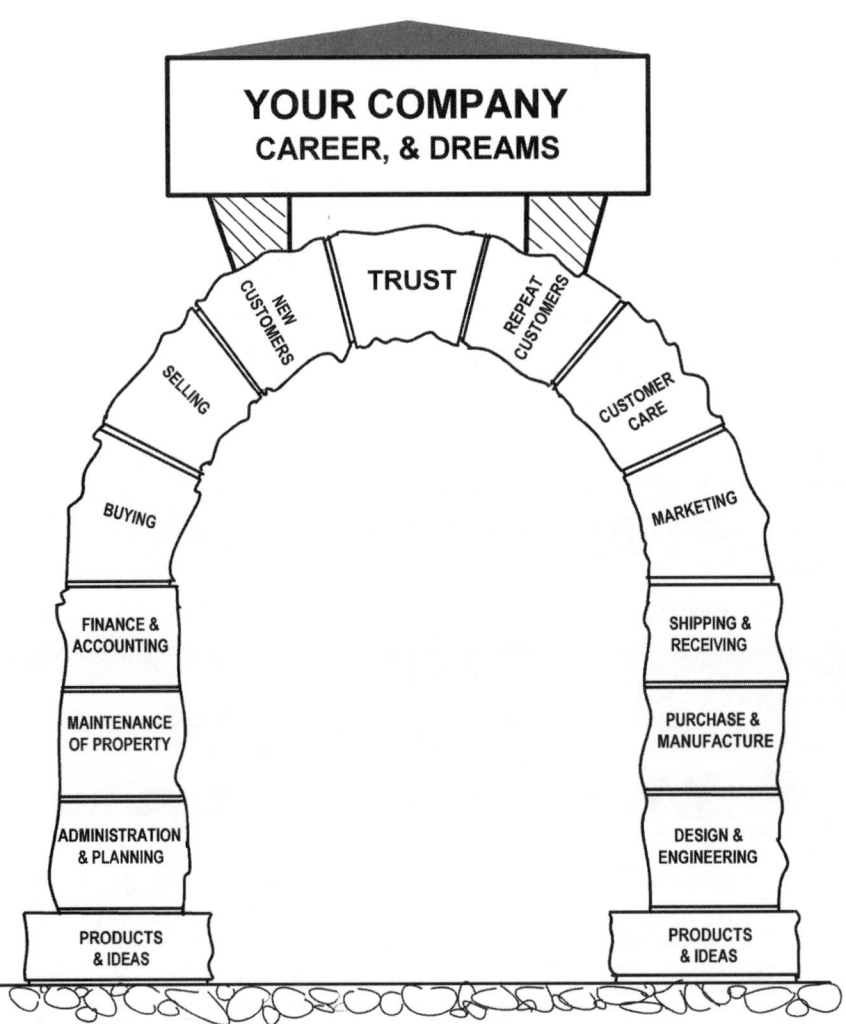

The Business Arch

The Business Arch

I grappled for days on end searching for a way to picture the interrelationships of the functions that exist in every business; then realized the arch was the answer.* Think of an arch supporting your business if you own it or the company you work in and are part of.

An arch is a very strong structure that gracefully supports a load when all the blocks are in place. So long as all blocks are viable it will stand strong without mortar or glue but when even one block weakens the arch falls; no matter how strong the mortar or glue. The blocks in the Business Arch are functions performed by people; e.g., you and I, in whatever company and organization we work in. We are the blocks in the Arch as we perform the functions of the block we are in at any point in time. We strengthen or weaken the block we are in by what we say and how we say it and what we do and how we do it.

The Arch is shown here with all major business functions. This volume of *The Perception Of A Difference* series gives you in-depth coverage of four: Buying, Marketing, Selling, and Customer Care. New customers appear throughout with their real life perceptions and reactions. Customer Care is in many of the stories. It sneaks in without your realizing it. Its importance is illustrated in Chapter 11. The role of Trust, the keystone of the Arch, is woven throughout the stories. You will recognize it even if you forget to look for it, but if you don't, Chapter 12's story will convince you of its importance.

---

*The noun form of business is used interchangeably with the noun company in this book.

Chapter 1

Making Dreams Come True

The sale of something is essential to the happiness of every individual and the existence

of every enterprise, be it business, educational, religious, political, or other. Important personal

endeavors, including choosing a marriage partner, maintaining a friendship, and getting a job

require selling. Selling requires a buyer, reaching the buyer requires marketing in some form,

and when the sale is made the customer must be cared for in a way that ensures s/he will

buy from the business again and also tell others to.

Buying, Marketing, Selling, and Customer Care are key blocks in the Arch of business

and personal success. They are held in place by Trust, the keystone in the Arch and

supported by Customers. You can't have any one without the others and they

all depend on the power of the perception of a difference.

The Perception Of A Difference (POD)

The very first time you saw or spoke with your best friend, you formed positive perceptions of each other. You have been strengthening those perceptions and making a difference to each other ever since. Those perceptions formed *without your conscious effort.* You justified them after they formed. The same process occurs the first time you walk into a restaurant, talk to a salesperson, accountant, attorney, candidate for office, or anyone. We make decisions and act upon them based on perceptions. That is the power of *The Perception Of A Difference.*

This book, and the others in the series, shows you how the *Perception Of A Difference* works in the interaction between someone who wants to buy and someone with something to sell. In every story the customer has a dream that the seller can make come true, while satisfying a dream of the seller in the process.

Making Dreams Come True

The perception of a difference gives you and me the power to make dreams come true. Your positive perception of a difference opens the door for you by causing others to accept you; after that, when you make a positive difference to them they make your dreams come true. You cannot make your dreams come true without the help of other people. It is always a cooperative effort, which fails when you and your team don't do the job you are capable of.

Almost every dream involves a buying process. Every buying process involves Marketing, Selling, and Customer Care. Different people participate in (or are responsible for) each one. The three functions are inextricably intertwined in bringing the buying process and the dream that triggered it, to a successful, happy conclusion. When this happens the dream that triggered it comes true, along with your dreams and the dreams of many other people.

Selling Is A Calling

I went into selling because I felt called to do so. I quickly found that I liked it and received much satisfaction from doing it successfully. The "high" of landing a sale and depositing the commission check was only part of it. I knew that something deeper and more important was creating my satisfaction and sense of usefulness. I didn't know what it was until...

We had landed a sale for a very large system. Its value exceeded my quota for the year by 52 percent. It was a record breaker for me and my team. It turned out to be a record breaker for the company. It took 18 months from the first face-to-face call to contract signing. After the third face-to-face call I was convinced that we could get the order if we did everything right. That called for planning, which we were used to as a team.

We stretched white wrapping paper along the length of one wall in the support team's office and fastened it with masking tape. On it we laid out our plan to land that order. At the far right end of the paper, at the top, we wrote a date 18 months in the future, under which we printed, "Contract Signing." Under that we put the name of the person who had the pen power to do it. Then we asked ourselves, "What is the last thing that must happen before he can sign?" The board of directors, or at least its finance committee, has to meet and approve it. We wrote that on the paper just to the left of contract signing and put a tentative date above it. Then we moved to the left of that entry and wrote down what had to happen before that meeting, and put a tentative date down. We continued that process until we had worked our way back to the current date at the far left end of the chart and wrote "Prepare Plan Chart."

That chart remained on the wall until after the contract was signed. The chart included who we would call on and when, for each week in the 18-month sales effort. If we didn't know a name, we put in the title of the person we knew or guessed would have to be involved. We knew it was an educational process so we listed the subjects that would be discussed and taught at each meeting. We listed the people who would do the teaching. We would do the lion's share of the work. We also would use district office people, the District Manager (my boss), experts from Headquarters Marketing, Headquarters Engineering, the Region Manager, and the Vice President of Customer Support. We informed each of these people that they would be needed, and we gave them an approximate date to put on their planning calendars. It took more than two days to complete the plan chart. We implemented it and kept adjusting the plan as we went along.

Eighteen months later, when I walked into our office with the signed contract, we celebrated and laughed and cried. I asked the receptionist to call us only if it was an emergency, and we all took two days off.

Six weeks later I was in headquarters for a meeting. On the second day the Vice President of Manufacturing asked me to join him when the day's sessions ended.

"I want to show you the assembly line for your system. I think you will find it interesting."

We arrived at the beginning of the line, and he introduced me to the person working at that point in the process and explained what was being done. He then took me to the next position and did the same thing. Each person I met was obviously and sincerely glad to meet and talk with me. They thanked me for getting the order and assured me they would build it properly. When we reached the end of the line I was impressed and moved. Then...

"You have given 50 families work for five months. I wanted you to meet them and let them tell you how much they appreciate it."

That hit me right between the eyes. I was instantly filled with a feeling best described as a combination of modesty and satisfaction. When I got to my hotel room later, I knelt and said "Thank you; now I know why I'm in sales and why it is so satisfying."

✧✧✧

If you are in sales now, have you had a similar experience?

My hunch is that you have and will remember it soon. If not, I'm sure you will. It will give you a sense of worth like no other.

For me selling became another calling; a work that was good and honorable because I helped others and made their lives better. In doing this I also earned a very good income and had a whale of a lot of fun. The hundreds of people I worked with enriched my life greatly.

We Made A Difference

A dream shared by three top management people triggered the process of buying that large system. They were responsible for the health of a large manufacturing company. They needed to slow rising costs and improve responsiveness to customers. This required better product design and improved customer care after the sale. If they could do this they would maintain competitive position and ensure continuing work for several hundred employees.

As a result of normal prospecting, I came on the scene at the time these discussions were in full swing and asked questions. When the third call ended, I was pretty certain that one of our systems would really help them to achieve their goals. The plan on the wall in our office was a plan for making them educate us fully and we to educate them fully. The plan chart had periodic checkpoints where we would check to be certain our system was right for them. At each checkpoint a "No" would have ended the effort.

Every person that came before the customer, in 18 months, made a difference. They strengthened and maintained the positive perception of a difference the buyers perceived. In landing the sale we made a difference to many people we would never see or know. In addition to the "50 families" and the customer's several hundred employees, there were the people who created the purchased parts in the system and the sales teams that sold them to our company and on and on. We helped their dreams and ours to come true. Buying, Marketing, Selling, and Customer Care intertwined to make it happen.

Buying, Marketing, Selling, and Customer Care are processes, a fact that may be surprising. Once I understood this, it enabled me to be more productive and increase my earnings with less effort per sale. It also made me a much wiser and savvy buyer. The processes function in every buying and selling situation; personal, retail, or wholesale. They function without our awareness.

The following chapters will show you these processes in action so you can be more successful in your life endeavors.

CHAPTER 2

Buying

Why have a chapter on Buying, in a book devoted to Marketing and Selling? This is a good question, considering that few sales training classes include it as a subject. My reason is simple: you will be much more effective selling and experience less unproductive selling time when you understand how you and everyone else makes the buying decision. My aim is to help you sell while standing in the prospect's (customer's) shoes. It makes a difference. The client, your customer, is outside looking in at everything you do in Marketing, Selling, and Customer Care. You can't see yourself. It would be wonderful if you could. This chapter will give you the opportunity.

We are buying and selling every day of our lives. Perceptions affect the decisions we make in these transactions because all decisions are based on perceived differences. They are our perception of the positive or negative difference (POD) of each person and company we have contact with. **These perceptions form in our minds without conscious thought or control.** They are created and influenced by you and others in your company; what they say and how they say it; what they do; and how they do it. All of this is involved in a process. When we understand the process we are in possession of a tool that can improve our own life and the lives of others.

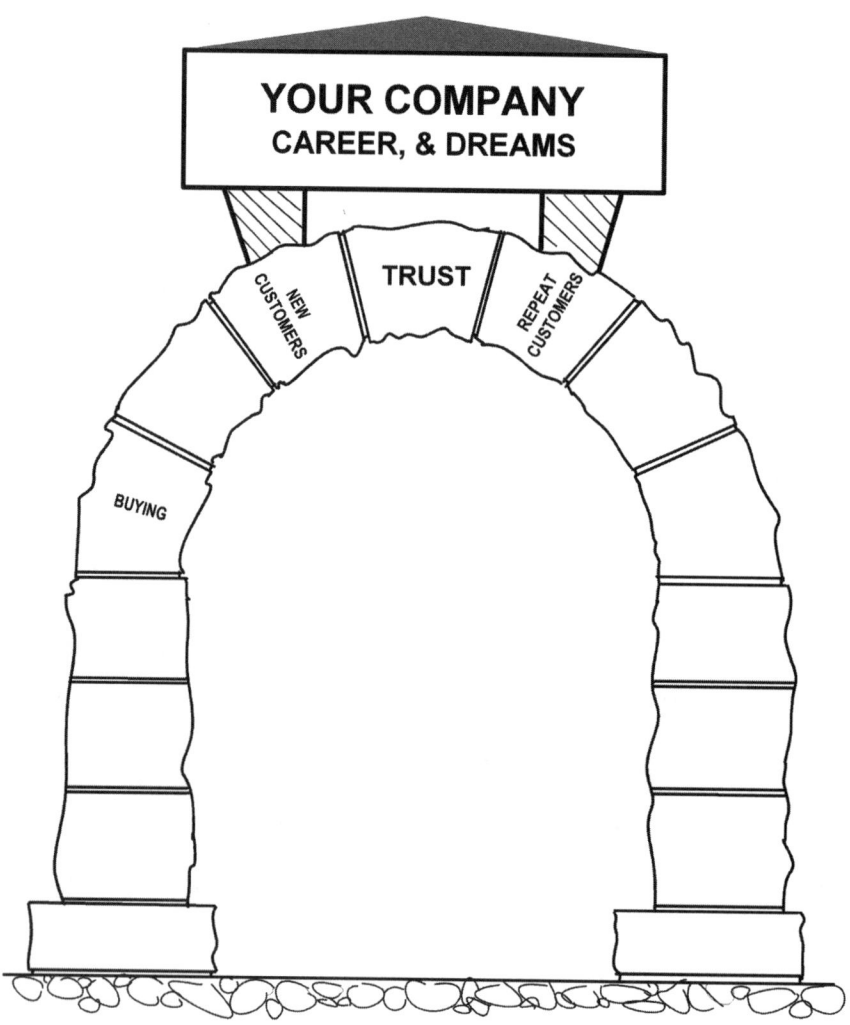

The Business Arch

Buying Is A Process

Buying is an educational process in which you, the buyer, are the student most of the time and the seller is the teacher. You need to know if and how the product will fit into your plans, your life.* The seller is the primary source of education on how the product works, in what circumstances, and

the results it produces. The seller provides this information on the label, on the package, in brochures, in a catalog, on the screen of whatever electronic device you are using, and through direct, interactive contact with a human.

The majority of your purchase decisions will be made without contacting a human representative of the seller. You set the pace of your education and you initiate the contact with a representative of the seller. Up to the time you contact a seller's representative, you are in complete control of the process; after contact you are subject to a variety of forces, which are illustrated in this and the next three chapters.

The Perception Of A Difference Is Always Involved

Your buying decision will be affected by everything you see and hear about the product and the seller from the first moment you begin the buying process. This includes the label on the product, the color and wording on the package, the way it is displayed on the shelf, the catalog page, or in the showroom. Tone of voice and body language communicate in person, on the radio, or in a television commercial. The message on the seller's web page and in e-mail messages carry a "tone" you will

---

*The word "product" is used throughout this book to denote both "hard" products; e.g., auto, razor, can of soup, and "services" of all kinds; e.g., landscaping, house painting, hair cutting, and styling.

sense. All of this affects your perception of the value of the product to you, your decision to buy, and who to buy from. Input from satisfied and unsatisfied users of the product and customers of the seller also will strongly influence your decision.

The Buying Process Consists Of Five Steps And A "Wild Card"

All five steps are executed for every purchase you and I make. The "wild card" does not appear in every purchase. One of the five steps, the most important from the seller's viewpoint, is partially completed in this story.

"I wouldn't buy from you if you were the last specialty office supply store in the world!"

My assistant said this loudly as she slammed the phone on the receiver. She was looking for a new place to set up an account since our old standby had closed its doors when the owner retired.

"What caused that reaction?"

"He doesn't respect women. His tone of voice and words said it all. He talked down to me."

"How did you find out about that place?"

"They had an attractive ad in the business directory."

What kind of Customer Care would you expect from this business?

What would have been different if the person on the phone had been the receptionist in the office of a doctor or an attorney or an accountant? They are sellers, also.

Was the perception of a difference at work here?

I ask these questions because people in these three professions often forget they are in business and subject to the same forces that affect other businesses. Business directory advertisements are not inexpensive. I know this from testing them to advertise my own business. This story clearly shows how an advertising investment can be made nonproductive just by answering the phone poorly. The business directory ad created a perception of a difference positive enough to cause this person to call the business. The person that answered the phone created a negative perception of a difference strong enough to completely overcome it.

The moral of this story is simple. Do not pick up the phone until you are prepared to be friendly, and have shed both your biases and your feeling of superiority.

Five Steps And The Wild Card

This story contains all five steps plus the "wild card," and illustrates the key function in the buying process.

"Wes, why did you buy this wine?"

"Because the label attracted me."

"And this one?"

"Because Ike, the wine department person, recommended it."

"We've drunk a lot of his recommendations, but buying because you liked the label... .

Did he also recommend this expensive bottle? It will blow my household budget right out the window."

"Actually, it's your fault. I started thinking about what you are fixing for dinner as I walked through the wine department on the way to get the milk you asked for and decided we should have wine with it. The first bottle was inexpensive. When I picked up the second to read the label, Ike talked about it so that went into the cart, also. Then I saw a shelf talker under this wine bin. The wine is rated 98 out of 100 by a famous wine critic and we've never tried it. The price seemed high, so I put it back."

"So why is it here now?"

"Remember, the dish you're fixing tonight is one I love, a special favorite of mine, and I finally decided we should try this wine with it. I didn't buy two other items I'd planned on getting, so the wine didn't seem so expensive. Besides, I know the winemaker that produced this wine."

"How long did it take you to figure this out?"

"About five minutes."

"When you go back for the milk, which you forgot, please don't buy any more wine!"

Without the "wild card" this story would not have happened.

Do you know what the wild card is?

Was the perception of a difference at work here?

If yes, when? How?

I did not go to the supermarket to buy wine. I went for the purpose of buying milk and a couple of other items that I didn't really need but had decided to buy anyway. I walked through the wine department because the store is laid out to make that the most logical route to the cheese and milk area after entering the store. I stopped to look at the label on the first bottle on impulse — the "wild card," which is involved in 55 to 60 percent of all buying decisions. As I did so I perceived a "want" as I thought about the dish Amy was preparing. I converted this want into a perceived need. I justified the need by checking the price, and seeing that it was low, I placed the bottle in the cart. After all, we can always afford a low-priced bottle of wine.

Picking up the second bottle was also an impulse. When Ike, whose judgment I trusted, recommended it I unconsciously went through the "want-to-need conversion." I justified the need because it would give us a choice of wines at dinner, put it in the cart, and headed for the milk cooler. The wine display is arranged so that the expensive fine wines are the last ones you pass on your way to the dairy area. That is where the shelf talker attracted my attention. At this point I was mentally tuned to thoughts of wine and the dish Amy was preparing had grown more special in my mind. This made it easy to perceive a want and convert it to a need while I examined this expensive bottle. Justifying the cost was harder, but putting off the purchase of the two items I didn't really need got me over that hurdle.

In a sense, I had decided whom I would buy from when I entered the store. It is our favorite grocery supermarket. The staff in this store has created and maintained a positive perception of a difference. In essence I bought the first bottle from the store, the second bottle from Ike, and the expensive one from the winemaker I had met and talked with a year earlier. He created a positive perception of a difference in my mind at that time.

Now do you see the five steps in the buying process?

You have been performing them all your life and just didn't realize it.

Buying Is A Five-Step Educational Process

The steps are:
1. You perceive a want.
2. You convert the want into a perceived need.
3. You decide who you will buy from when/if you actually complete a purchase.
4. You justify the need and the purchase obligations.
5. You justify your choice of whom you will buy from.

These five steps may take place over a period as long as several years, or as short as 30 seconds, but you always do them. Every week you perceive many wants that quickly disappear from your mind. The wants that become needs are those you are reminded of frequently and have a perceived value in your life. In step four you make the decision to buy now or conclude that you don't really need it or that it can wait for a future time. These delayed purchases can lay dormant in the back of your mind for years before you act on them.

You decide whom to buy from without conscious thought and it remains in force throughout the dormancy period for a delayed purchase. This decision can begin during the process of perceiving a want. It is usually completed during step two when you are educating yourself; "kicking tires," getting prices, and thinking about budget impact. This was the case for my wife's friend in the next story. I strongly suspect that she made the decision to buy from the people who got her business, when she first went into their store and talked with them.

The decision about who to buy from is strongly based on the positive or negative perception that forms when you first contact (or are contacted by) people at sources for the product or service. These contacts can be a voice in a radio ad, a face in a TV ad, a phone conversation, when a salesperson walks into your office, or the first time you walk into a place of business. The perception that forms on that first contact is powerful and automatic. You may not be conscious of it or admit it to yourself at that point in the buying process. It is the perception of a difference and its longevity is amazing.

The Key Function In The Buying Process

I have not mentioned the key function of the buying process. It is clearly shown in this conversation between my wife and a friend of hers.

"I've spent a year thinking about new countertops, looked in at least ten stores to get ideas and information on different materials and prices. Now I'm going to put in granite tile."

"I saw a big tile store on Camille Street last week. Have you been there?"

"Yes, just two days ago. The building is impressive and the front doors told me their prices would be high, but I went in anyway. They have a tremendous, beautifully displayed selection of countertop, floor, and wall materials in tile, stone, and solid ceramics, but I will not give them my business because every associate I met or heard talking to other customers was haughty. Only haughty people would enjoy buying there. I'll get the same quality granite from the smaller place a block away because the people think I'm important."

"How do you know that?"

"From the way they talk with me."

"How are their prices?"

"I don't know. Whatever they are I'll buy there, and those people are going to install it. They were nice to me months ago, and they were today."

Moral: You make a difference with everything you do and say, usually without being aware of it.

Five groups of people created a perception of a difference in this story.
- The owner/partners of the store with the big selection.
- The architect that designed that store.
- The associates in that store.
- The customers in that store.
- The "people" in the other store.

The owner/partners of the big store either discussed their business model with the architect or gave him a copy of their business plan. The architect designed the store to send a message of superior quality and staying power based on input from one or both of these sources. *"The building is impressive and the front doors told me their prices would be high but I went in anyway."* This comment indicates the design achieved its goal.

Architects attest to the fact that the space we live and work in affects our attitude and outlook on life. This and the attitude of the owners resulted in the perception the associates created in the mind of my wife's friend. She described them as "haughty," another word for arrogant, an attitude of superiority.

What interested me when I listened to the story is the fact that the customers conveyed the same attitude. Their perception of the store and staff was not negative. They were either accustomed to this ambiance and attitude or enjoyed the prestige of shopping there. In any event they contributed to the negative perception in the mind of my wife's friend.

The competitor's "people" created and maintained a positive perception of a difference and got the business. Price was not a deciding factor, people were. What sticks out in this story, in addition to the effect of the perception of a difference, that was not obvious in the two preceding stories?

Education!

She could not make a buying decision until she educated herself enough to decide which countertop material would fit her needs, her lifestyle. She had visited many kitchen design and remodeling stores asking questions and picking up brochures to learn about the various countertop materials and their properties. It was during the education step in the buying process that she decided who would get her business whenever she was able to do it. *"They were nice to me months ago."* This comment indicates the decision was made subconsciously early in the process.

She obviously perceived a want and then over time it became a need. The next step was to learn which material was best for her. Later, when her countertop installation was completed, she was completely satisfied and happy with the result, just as I was when we drank the expensive bottle of wine with that special dish.

The winemaker had educated me about his winemaking style and its results long before I read the label on the bottle in the store. My wife's friend had spent months educating herself, and it had been a year since I had met and talked with the winemaker. In both cases the purchase seemingly died when in reality it was only in step two of the buying process. When you fail to learn enough about a product and how you will use it before completing the purchase the result is "buyer's remorse." The bigger the price tag the greater the "remorse" potential.

The New Motorcycle

This story shows the multitude of factors involved in a buying decision.

I drove a standard size, two-cylinder motorcycle for seven years during my youth. Amy rode on it with me when we courted because it was my only transportation. I always thought it would be fun to have one again but put it out of my mind. Last year my across-the-street neighbor, ten years younger than me, bought a used six-cylinder touring motorcycle. To me it is a monster. I watched him practice with it, up and down the street. He also owned a cycle when he was younger. Somehow, watching him made me acutely aware of every motorcycle that passed me on the street, particularly a new re-creation of my old motorcycle.

Amy shared my dream of riding two wheels again so we finally went to a dealership three miles from our home and looked at cycles. I sat on the re-creation of my old bike, and fell in love: Amy did, too. This cycle has the same front suspension and color scheme as the one I rode while courting her. She said she'd like a cycle again just for fun rides on the back roads. I allowed as how I could ride it to some client meetings.

Amy walked around the big showroom looking at other models and the clothing display. I sat on the bike and tried to talk with the salesperson. He was not too attentive, and he gave me the feeling (perception) that either he did not know the answers to my questions or didn't want to take the time to tell me about new features compared to the machine of my youth. When Amy returned, I thanked him for his time and as we drove home…

"Maybe you should stop in at this dealership regularly and look for a good deal on a used cycle."

"Nope! I won't buy from that dealership."

"I expected you to say that. I didn't feel comfortable with them, either."

I started searching the web for motorcycle information. I wanted to know what had changed in the equipment, laws, and driving considerations. Also, I needed to know how a motorcycle navigates on interstate highways that are heavily traveled by semi-trucks. I gave myself an education on the Internet, but that wasn't the same as talking with someone.

Six months later in the paper's "what's happening around town" column, we read about a free seminar on proper maintenance of a motorcycle and safe driving practices. It was to be at a dealership for the make I love, 18 miles away. I went to it.

It was a great, informative seminar, attended by over a hundred riders. It completed the education I needed to decide if I would enjoy a motorcycle again. Something about the people in the dealership and the willingness of the owner and service manager to talk to me made me decide to buy from them when we can afford it.

Before I bought I took the three-day beginner's course in motorcycle riding. It is recommended by the state Motor Vehicle Department and was strongly endorsed by everyone I met at the dealer seminar. I got my motorcycle driver's license, and I bought riding apparel and the cycle from them, a 36-mile round trip from home. I have complete confidence in them.

✧✧✧

When was the decision of who to buy from made?

Does that support the earlier statement that we decide who to buy from before we are certain we will buy the product?

Which dealer's people gave the most caring, sincere Customer Care?

We decided where we would not buy on our first visit to a dealer. Our purpose in going there was to be educated about the product. The decision about whom we would buy from was made on our first visit to another dealer. At the time those decisions were made we could not possibly afford a motorcycle. We were in the educational portion of the buying process. We had a want. We did not have a need or any willingness to convert the want into a need.

Note that Amy and I are completely happy with the decision to buy from a dealer 18 miles from home when the same motorcycle and apparel were available at the same price in a dealership only three miles from home. That would be the case even if I were not writing this book about the power of the perception of a difference.

Why?

Because of perceptions created by people.

The first dealer's people created a negative perception in our minds. The second dealer's people created a strong positive perception. The first dealer will never get the chance to change the negative perception. The second dealer got the business plus good references from us. We are already telling people about the experience. Wouldn't you do the same?

Price Versus The Perception Of A Difference

Twenty plus years of consulting and research have convinced me that cost is only important when it is completely out of sync with our income. Before credit cards were invented, you and I would have delayed a purchase until we had saved enough money to pay for it. In the case of real estate or a means of transportation, we might save enough to make the down payment and then sign a mortgage or installment payment agreement. These were items for which we had a compelling need. Most other purchases were made after we had saved enough for them.

We did not buy much on credit because setting up a credit account took time. We knew the majority of our creditors personally, a fact that caused us to make sure we made payments on time. But even then, price/cost only helped determine the quality level of the product or delayed the purchase, it did not determine who we would buy from.

Now, as then, our perception of the person(s) and the establishment is the deciding factor in who we will buy from. The price of a product plays even less of a role now because money is instantly available with the credit instruments in our pockets. The stories above clearly support this. The perception created by people makes the difference. This is true in large and small purchases. In the granite tile story, when Amy asked her friend about the role of price in her decision she said, "I don't know. Whatever it is, I'll buy there."

Price is typically fourth in importance in our buying decision process. It becomes a tiebreaker when all other things are equal, but all things are never equal because two people or two sales teams can rarely create the same level of trust and likeability in our minds. Any price can be justified when we like the people and are sufficiently educated about the product in relation to our perceived needs.

Any Price Can Be Justified

If you don't believe this, read on.

Money was tight at the time that the lease on the car was nearing expiration. We had owned many large cars. We had leased this small one as an experiment. With the children grown up and married we wondered if a large car was justified for our purposes. I came to like the small car and its maneuverability. The fuel mileage at 32 miles per gallon, average, was great. I thought my wife liked it, too. Until…

"I think I'd like a bigger car again."

"We can't afford it now, Honey. You know that because you pay all the monthly bills."

"TV ads all claim that great deals can be had at this time. Why don't you talk to the manager at the dealer where we had the last big car serviced? You always liked them."

"I'll think about it."

Of course, this approach got me nowhere fast. I did look at ads, and I even stopped in to look at cars in two dealerships, being careful to not leave my card lest they pester me to death because I wasn't ready to buy yet. In both cases I left with neutral perceptions of how they would be to deal with.

After three more days of badgering from my wife, I went to the dealer who had serviced our last big car. There I looked at, and got educated about, a luxury version of the small car we had. It had a different model name and some features ours didn't. I knew it would be dependable because the same maker built the last three cars we'd owned. I liked it and took home brochures. I also took pricing on the big cars this dealer sold as well as a firm proposal on the luxury small one. I liked and trusted the people in this dealership. Their service and the attitude of the service department people on our old big car was outstanding.

I gave all the information to my wife and started my sales effort.

"The small car gives us the luxury features and appointments we've had in big cars and keeps the advantages of high gas mileage and handling that I like."

"But it just doesn't feel the same, not as secure."

"We can't afford it."

"Maybe if I talked to the manager we could get a better deal."

"OK, I'll make an appointment to do a test drive of the small car and after that you can talk to whoever you want to."

We went; we drove the luxury small car; she liked it and I liked it. We took the big car for a test drive. Actually, she drove it. We both liked it, also. We left with an appointment to come back in three days and take delivery of the luxury small car. Three days later we drove away in the big beauty.

In three days my wife had:
- Reworked the budget.
- Postponed some purchases that had been real needs.
- Convinced the dealer's manager that he could sharpen his pencil on both the total amount and the monthly payment schedule.
- Gotten him to provide the color and upholstery she wanted even though he did not have it in stock.

More to my amazement, she had justified a $10,226 difference in price and two extra years of monthly payments. Her explanation:

"I really want a big car and I really trust the people in that place."

✧✧✧

In another chapter I'll tell you about a different situation in which the price difference was 35 percent.* In it as in this story, a positive perception of a difference created the trust needed to justify the price.

---

*See Chapter 11.

By the way, the wild card impulse did not enter into my wife's buying decision. She told me afterward that it was her intention to get the big car all along if she could justify the cost difference in her own mind, my desires and opinion notwithstanding.

Prove It To Yourself

You may still be reluctant to believe that the perception of a difference is so powerful versus price. If this is the case, prove it to yourself. Look back on several purchases of importance to you. Now write down the history of that decision. Where your first impulse was "I can't afford it," how did you justify the eventual purchase? Interesting, isn't it? Amy and I eventually justified buying the re-creation of the motorcycle I courted her on at a time when mathematics and logic said we could not afford it.

Also, just for fun, after your next four trips to the supermarket, or just shopping trips, compare the items you came home with to items on the list you carried with you when you started your shopping trip. Four trips should prove that impulse, "the wild card," was involved in some way in over 50 percent of your purchases and you were able to justify them all.

Be Aware Of Influencers

Influencers affect the buying process almost as much as salespeople. They often do it without conscious intent and without our being aware that we have been influenced.

Ike was an obvious influencer in my decision to buy the expensive bottle of wine. He was not selling; the winemaker who made it was. Ike only told me how much he liked it. He had no personal interest in which wine I purchased.

The shelf talker influenced me. It was created and put there by the wine distributor's salesperson that set up the wine display. Both Ike and the distributor are agents of the winemaker, but I did not think about that at the time.

My wife's friend was influenced by the design of one building and by the conversations she heard between the customers and sales associates in the building. She may have been more influenced by that than the sales associates she talked with directly without being aware of it.

My neighbor influenced me simply by buying a motorcycle.

My wife influenced me to look into big cars in a very forceful way.

All of these influencers affected buying decisions. In each of these stories, the storyteller was influenced by information from external sources—some good, some bad. The outcome in each case was a combination of these external sources and the way they were perceived by the buyer. The fact that, except for the associates in the tile store, none of these people were "salespeople" is an important fact to keep in mind. You can also influence someone else's buying process for better or for worse by providing the right or wrong information at the right or wrong time.

Now Put On Your Seller's Hat

Buying and selling are personal processes, which you can perform more wisely when you stay aware of where you are in them: both as a buyer and a seller. You are in the selling process when you ask someone for a date and the buying process when you agree to it. You are in both processes when you change jobs or careers. You are selling your ability to make a worthwhile contribution to the employer. You are buying when you are deciding which company or person you want to work with.

Remember the five steps in the buying process and the power of the perception of a difference. Think about what is happening the next time you are buying and make certain you are fully educated before you complete the purchase. This is absolutely essential.

When you are on the seller's side of the buying decision, think about the steps the buyer must complete. Ask yourself, have I provided everything the buyer needs at each point in those five steps? Have I insulted the buyer's intelligence or not told enough with my marketing message or during this face-to-face sales discussion? In the chapters that follow you will listen to people in Marketing, Selling, and Customer Care as they win and lose sales. Please keep the five buying steps in mind as you do.

Marketing, the purpose of which is first to influence, then educate, and finally to sell is the subject of the next chapters. You will find it fascinating and interesting now that you understand the buying process.

Chapter 3

Marketing

A Key Block In The Business Arch

The Arch that supports every business organization, and the jobs of everyone in it, cannot stand

without marketing. Accepting any job in Marketing is accepting great responsibility. Carrying that

responsibility requires consistent honesty in everything marketing says, prints, and does.

This requires the support and honesty of everyone in the organization.

Marketing's function and responsibilities in a business are widely misunderstood.

I came to this realization as I worked with both owners of

small businesses and top management in large corporations.

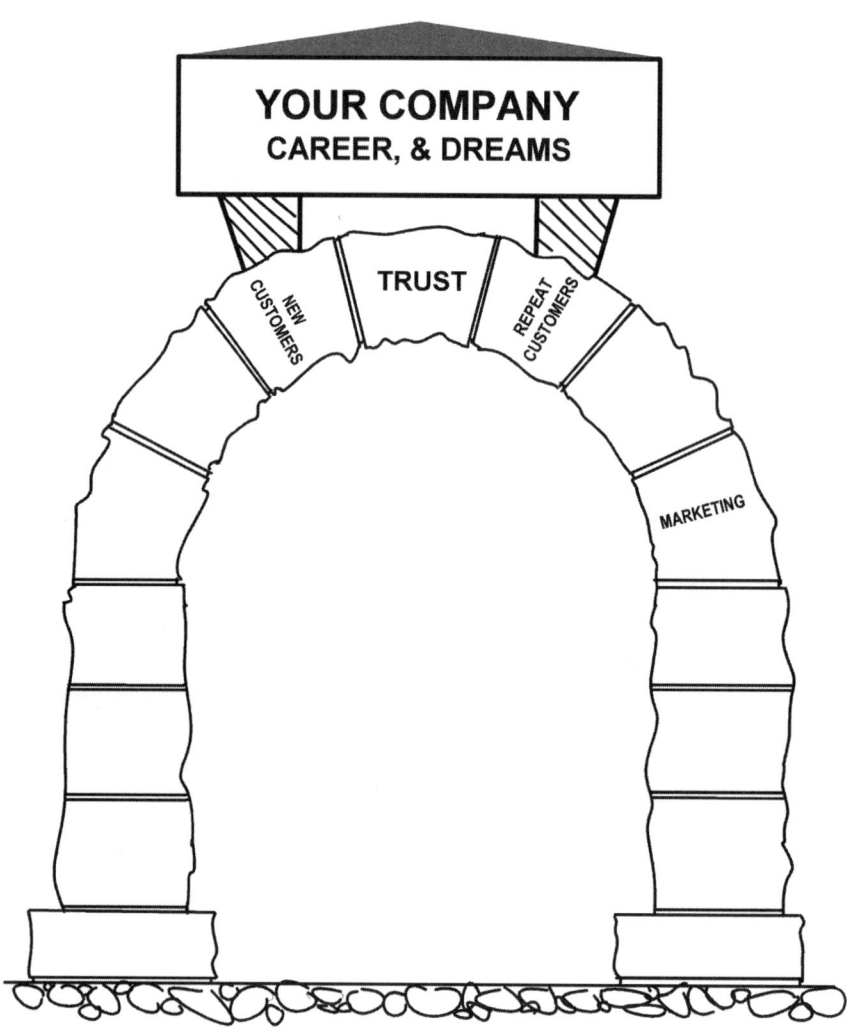

YOUR COMPANY
CAREER, & DREAMS

NEW CUSTOMERS

TRUST

REPEAT CUSTOMERS

MARKETING

The Business Arch

The misunderstanding derives from two premises:

1. Marketing and selling are the same.

2. Marketing's major function is advertising.

Both of these premises are incorrect.

Marketing and selling are educational processes but they deliver the education in totally different ways. The key difference is this: Marketing educates the buyer without active interaction between the buyer and seller; selling educates the buyer with active interaction between the buyer and salesperson. This interaction can be face-to-face, oral using voice communication technology, written using instant electronic communication, or any combination of the three.

Marketing also educates the salesperson about the product and the results of its use. If the education from Marketing is sufficient for the buyer to make a buying decision no additional selling is needed.

A Multifaceted Education Process

Observation of and research into business organizations that have enjoyed long-term success shows that their management understands the true, larger role of Marketing. In these companies Marketing is involved in essentially all business decisions. It is the source of decision data with or without recommendations for action. It is often the decision implementer. It is the educator of people inside and outside the organization. Truly, Marketing determines the success of every business organization, and it does it using the perception of a difference.

During the early life of a small business, marketing functions are performed by one person, usually the founder. As the business grows those functions and responsibilities are passed to other people who eventually become the Marketing operation of the organization.

Marketing educates the designer, engineer, and entrepreneurial thinker about a product while it is in the conceptual stage. At this point it educates these people about the need for the product, if one exists, and what the need requires in product capability. It then educates you and me. It may educate us directly or through salespeople at several stages of the distribution process. Depending on the product, this can include the company's salespeople, distributors, distributor salespeople, customer care people, and installers.

Marketing helps us make the buying decision that is correct for our needs, the one most likely to make our dreams come true. Its task is to make us aware of the product's existence and make the buying process easy and satisfying. It accomplishes this through education and training. Education helps us to learn "why;" training helps us to learn "how."

To educate people, Marketing must use the tools that teachers use: questions, visual aids, and oral presentations in a dialog with us, and everyone that helps in our education. The dialog is carried on using the communication tools that are appropriate and effective. Marketing sets the price of the product; educates you and me on the appropriateness of the price; and it adjusts the price from time to time based on what it learns from us in the ongoing dialog.

Marketing does not create wants. It creates awareness of a product's existence, capability, and availability, and plays a role in our discovery of wants and needs not satisfied by existing products. If the product is an alternative to an existing product, Marketing creates the perception of a positive difference that will cause us to consider buying it instead of the competing product.

All of the above make up the fascinating scope of Marketing. The size of the producer, price of the product, its size, simplicity, or complexity do not change the purpose and scope of Marketing. Only the details and time required for execution change. In a small business, all of these tasks may be performed by one individual and gradually divided among others as the business grows.

Should We Add This To Our Product Line?

Management should ask Marketing this question when a product idea is first conceived: when Marketing begins educating for a new product. To answer it, Marketing must get the answers to 27 questions. Answers to the first 16 will come from the individuals and teams most capable of discerning them, including the conceiver, engineers, designers, manufacturing people, cost accountants, and salespeople. Marketing will develop answers to the remaining questions. The answers must be well researched and accurate because much effort, expense, and heartache will result if they are not.

Answer These Questions

1. How soon will new technology make the product obsolete or unnecessary?
2. How soon can production quantities be on the shipping dock?
3. What must the buyer do to install and use this product?
4. What will this cost the buyer in addition to the purchase price?
5. What does this product do?
6. What does this do for the buyer?
7. Of what value is this to the buyer?
8. What percentage of this value is quantifiable; how much is perceived?
9. What does the buyer do or use to obtain this value currently?
10. Is this clearly a better way or just an alternate choice among many?
11. If clearly a better or totally new way, how quickly will competitors appear?
12. If an alternate choice, why should it be perceived as preferable?
13. What is the expected useful life of this product?
14. Will the buyer need or want a replacement when it wears out?
15. Is it important that the product be durable, or just maintainable?
16. What will it cost to put the product on the shipping dock?

If the product has survived these questions, Marketing develops answers to these next questions.

17. How many potential buyers exist?
18. Where are they located, in what density in each location?
19. How do these buyers usually learn about the existence of a product like this?

20. What will it cost to make them aware of its existence?
21. What will the buyer need to learn during the buying process?
22. Who will do the educating?
23. How will the education be delivered?
24. What will be the delivered cost of the education?
25. What price to the buyer will make the product profitable to all involved?
26. Why will the buyer be willing to pay this price?
27. When, after product introduction, will price become primary in the buying decision?

Based on the answers to these 27 questions, the product is either shelved or approved for production and sale.

Question 1 is the most important in today's modern world. In years past it might never have been asked. If the time quoted in the answer to Question 1 is short, there may be no need to ask any other questions.

The answer to Question 2 will either support the decision to shelve, or become important when compared to the answers to the rest of the questions. In any event, these questions must be asked very early in the creation phase of every product. Their answers come long before the development of a Marketing Plan. These questions should be asked about every product, by every potential investor in the product, or the company planning to produce it. In the process of answering them, Marketing is educating everyone concerned.

Consultants love to compare war stories; here are some that I remember. They show exactly how important the questions are.

Ask Question 1 Repeatedly

My client had written a software package that stored and retrieved photographic quality images. It was unique in its compressing and decompressing capabilities and the way these were applied. The image was compressed before being written to the data storage medium. When retrieved, the compressed image was shown on the monitor screen. This enabled the user to retrieve and look at many images at once and select for decompression and full size viewing only those desired. This saved the user a lot of time. The software also had clever database search capabilities that provided the user with great flexibility. The product could be used in medical facilities, mail order catalogs, law enforcement, prisons, and essentially anywhere that images were important. It was a dream product.

Initially it used TV cameras to capture the images. When digital cameras arrived, the product was quickly adapted to use them as well. Digital cameras were more expensive than TV cameras when first available but very flexible and intuitive to use. The client assumed they were no threat to the product since no computer software was offered with the digital cameras. Bad assumption....

The speed of digital camera improvement was blinding. The second round of digital cameras included storage and retrieval software at no extra charge. This software was crude in comparison to my client's product, but potential buyers were confident that the third round of digital cameras would include improved software. They waited, rather than buy my client's software because digital camera flexibility and intuitive use was so desirable. Digital camera manufacturers did not disappoint them. My client's dream product was dead.

A lot of people lost a lot of money on this product because question number one was not researched early enough in the product development cycle. I was hired when development was considered complete. If the question had been re-asked and answered, with adequate research at regular intervals during product development, it could have become clear that the real product was the client's software. He then could have sold it, or the rights to it, to one of the digital product manufacturers and received a good return on all his effort. He didn't think of these manufacturers as possible competitors and therefore did not research and analyze their capabilities.

Competitor research and analysis must be an ongoing project. It should include all known competitors and any others who have a stake in the technologies currently involved in your products. The research should also look for other technologies that may become involved. The early positive acceptance of the concept of computer stored retrievable images was well publicized. Companies developing digital cameras sent their salespeople to my client to sell cameras to him. They observed what the software accomplished for the user and reported it to their headquarters.

The moral is clear: regular, repeated research on emerging technologies and their possible use, tested against Question 1, is essential to success in today's business world.

Don't Forget Three And Four

Just answering Question 1 isn't enough as this story shows.

In the early years of computers, the most widely used brand had a software flaw which required execution of a time-consuming manual procedure every time each program was run. It had been necessary in this brand's earliest computers because of the limitations of their technology. It was not changed later when technology arrived that should have made it obsolete. It remained a thorn in the side of users even after they had purchased newer models.

An excellent engineer came up with a plug-in hardware solution that eliminated the procedure. He and his investors had put a lot of money into its development and the manufacture of several units before discovering that they were not selling. One of my clients referred them to me for help.

I examined their marketing plan. It told me exactly what the product did and its value to the user. Clearly, by their arithmetic, the product would pay back its purchase price in less than four months. I asked for one unit, which I took to the top man in the computer operation of another of my clients. If it worked for them, they would buy three units and we would give them the trial unit in exchange for their help.

In two weeks they gave it back to me. They discovered that they would have to modify every computer program that used this product. Furthermore, once the new hardware was installed, it would not run a mix of modified and unmodified programs. The required modifications made its use prohibitively expensive.

When I reported this to my client and his investors, he admitted that they had not thought of this. I assumed they had tried the product in a real life production situation. I was wrong.

The moral of this story is always answer Questions 3 and 4.

Marketing is teacher and consultant to management while asking these questions and verifying the accuracy of the answers. When the product is approved for further development and sale, Marketing becomes responsible for its success in the marketplace. This is a high-risk task because the devil is in the details. This makes planning essential.

The Product Marketing Plan

With the product approved, *Marketing's task is simply to make potential buyers aware of the product's existence and then make the buying process easy and satisfying.* A lifetime of experience and the input of several hundred people yielded this simple and profound insight. This requires a plan of action, which is most often referred to as a Product Marketing Plan. The best way to build the plan is to start at the end of the buying process for a product and work back to the present. The methodology is found in the story of the sale that gave 50 families work for five months.

The end point is when the buyer signs a contract, or purchase order, or says, "I'll take it" and selects a method of payment while walking to the cash register. This is the first point entered in the Marketing Plan. Coming back from each point, record all the things the buyer must learn to reach that point and each education task that must be completed. Identify the person responsible for each part of the education, and you will have completed the majority of the marketing plan. Remember that the last item you enter in the plan for the buyer's education is making the buyer aware of the existence of the product. *Experience shows that when this is the first thing thought about and recorded, the product is headed for very deep yogurt.* A buyer with awareness and no education will never buy.

It's All About Buyer Education

We began this discussion in Chapter 2 with the buying process and proved that a buyer, e.g., you and me, will not buy any product until we have educated ourselves sufficiently about the product's capabilities in relation to our needs. We must feel comfortable with the decision to buy it. We also learned that our education includes what we read on the product label or box, the comments of friends, articles and advertisements on calendars, in newspapers, magazines, newsletters, Internet, radio and TV media, and presentations by salespeople.

To be sure, we must first know of the product's existence, but that is the first step in a five-step process. The other steps can take 30 seconds or several years. Those 30 seconds or several years will involve the education of everybody on the buying committee, which invariably has more members than you thought it did. Therefore…

The Marketing Plan Is An Educational Plan

If the product is to be sold off the shelf without face-to-face or other interaction between the buyer and another person, Marketing will prepare the package design, illustrations, and text to be printed on the package. This must educate the potential buyer enough to make a buying decision possible.

Marketing will also prepare educational literature/brochures that may be posted or placed for pickup near the shelf with the product and shelf talkers. Shelf talkers are those small signs that appear below or above the product in the display. Designed to trigger an impulse to buy, they are often prepared by the store or distributor using forms prepared by Marketing.

When the product is a service, the package is the people who perform it, the equipment that is used in performing it, and the means by which the people and equipment arrive at the customer's site. You will see most of these items and their effect on the buyer in the landscape service story in this chapter. The opening page of this book also describes the marketing and selling of a service.

If the potential buyer cannot learn enough about the product to make the buying decision without interacting with another person, Marketing has a bigger job. In this case, it must educate the people who will interact with the buyer. With some products this can be accomplished with written communication in the form of white papers, data sheets, and lists of frequently asked questions with the correct answers. The role of the person contacted by the buyer is to interpret the data that is available to the buyer and help him in understanding its meaning and application to his situation. This is the role often played by the "inside" salesperson.*

This education assistance is relatively easy to do when the buyer is a single individual. However, the buyer is rarely the only person who will be affected by the purchase of a product.

---

*See Chapter 10 for explanation of "inside" salesperson and history of term.

Marketing's task is to make the education process easy and simple. This means the education process must be easy and simple for the buyer *and anyone the buyer may need for help in completing the education*. The Product Marketing Plan defines the amount of education that will be needed and the method of delivery that will make it easiest and simplest for the buyer to absorb. The method of delivery depends on the total number of facts, thought, and discussion necessary for the buyer to place the product in the context of his/her wants and needs. If this will fit on the product label, or the label and the package it is contained in, that is the method of education delivery. This is effective with easy-to-use products. As the product's use becomes more complex or the number of people involved in its use grows, the buying process becomes more complex and additional material may be required.

Services must be considered complex products for two reasons:
1. They are usually performed by more than one individual.
2. Results of the service tend to affect multiple people.

Each person in the team delivering the service must be educated and trained to ensure the results meet the customer's expectations. The customer is every person affected by the results. Our son is a single customer, but a new hairstyle created for him was the subject of considerable discussion during one family gathering. Fortunately for our son's peace of mind the number who did not like his new hairstyle were in the minority. A housecleaning service, however, must produce results that meet the expectations of everyone living in the house.

The Product Marketing Plan must identify the possible complexity and present an appropriate method of delivery. In selecting the appropriate delivery method, it will help if you substitute your product for the ones in the following discussions.

A Hermit's Beans

An example of a very simple buying process would be the purchase of a can of beans by a hermit when it was the only can of beans or any other edible product on the shelf of the only trading post within one or more days walking distance of his cabin.

How many decisions are involved in the hermit's purchase of the can of beans?

How much education does the hermit need to make the buying decision?

Beyond "Ready to eat, and serve, hot or cold," will the message on the label be of much importance?

In the context of the hermit's situation as described, the choices are:

• I'll take it.

• I prefer to starve.

Now consider the situation with three different cans of beans on the shelf, all at the same price, either three different versions of one brand or three different brands. Assume that the hermit has no credit at this trading post and only enough cash to buy one can of beans. Assume that he has never eaten any of the three kinds before… but he's hungry and has walked a long way to get a can of beans.

Is the buying process still simple?

Is the message on the labels of much importance?

What does the hermit need to learn from the labels to bring the buying process to a satisfactory conclusion?

Will he turn to the trading post owner and ask, "Which is the best-tasting brand?"

What would you do if you were the hermit?

What would you, as a marketing person, put on the label to ensure that your brand is purchased when the other brands are competitors? That's your responsibility, you know.

The buying process is not completely simple, as you will learn in a moment. The hermit's main decision will be which of the three cans to buy since he has only enough money to buy one. The labels will hopefully communicate enough information to make his decision more than a guess. If it were me, I would ask the trading post owner; but I am not a hermit. It's possible that hermits are hermits because they don't like to talk with people and above all else do not want to reveal ignorance. Assuming this is the case the label had better be communicative or the hermit will be frustrated and angry. This may be laughable but read on and learn how serious it really can be.

A Real Life Bean Purchase

Three weeks ago I went to the supermarket with the task of selecting food for my wife and me for dinner. The hot rotisserie chicken looked appealing so I put one in my cart. I considered accompaniments. I tasted samples of the coleslaw, potato salad, and baked beans. None of these hit the spot, but baked beans that really tasted good became a need. In the canned food aisle I found a brand we liked but had not had in a long time. I reached for a can.

The display had an array of six different flavors. I impulsively picked up the one labeled, "Original" then decided I had better check out the others. It took ten minutes to read all the labels and select the "Barbecued" version. The display was all mixed up by shoppers before me that had also read the different labels and didn't put the cans back where they picked them up. My chicken had gotten cold in the cart and I was angry by the time I checked out. We delayed dinner while the chicken was re-heated in the oven. Thankfully, the beans tasted good enough that we may try that flavor again.

Two days ago I observed and timed a woman doing the same selection effort comparing different brands of another "simple" food product. It added eight minutes to her shopping trip. She was mired in the buyer education process.

What made the hermit's buying process different than my bean purchase and the woman's purchase?

There were more people involved. The hermit, by definition, was a lone buyer. I was eating with my wife and had to consider her tastes in the selection decision. The woman wore a diamond and a wedding band and was the right age to have children at home. Her decision potentially affected several people, so it probably wasn't her decision alone. She and I only appeared to be alone. The invisible people in our lives made the buying process complex. The complexity of the buying process increases as the number of people affected by the purchase increases.

As a Marketing person, answer this question;

Was the variety of flavors within the same brand a wise marketing decision?

The complexity of the buying process increases as the number of decision makers increases. The number of decision makers is governed by the number of people that are individually responsible for the purchase of the product. The following vignette, based on an actual conversation, illustrates this very well.

Soup For Dinner

It had been a long day on the road, driving in a car with four children, ages five to nine….

"Hon, I am not up to fixing a meal when we get home. I suggest we stop at the supermarket close to home and buy enough canned soup for all of us."

"Vegetable beef or beef noodle sounds good to me."

"It's too hot for such heavy soup, chicken noodle is it."

"Why are we stopping at the store? I want to go home."

"We are having canned soup for dinner so I don't have to cook a lot."

"Vegetable beef is my choice, Mom."

"What do you want, Dad?"

"Dad already asked for vegetable beef or beef noodle and I vote for chicken noodle."

"Then let's make three kinds of soup and satisfy everyone, Mom."

"No, I am not getting three pots dirty this evening. We will have one kind of soup and I selected chicken noodle."

"You heard Mom: one kettle, one kind of soup. Let's get into the store and pick it out."

"If we are only having one, make it vegetable beef, please."

"It has peas, Judy. Mark won't eat it cause he doesn't eat peas."

"That's OK, I'll just pick the peas out and enjoy the rest. Paul can pick out the lima beans. That's what we always do with stuff we don't like."

"You two are trying to make up to Dad for all the trouble you were on the road, but it won't help tonight. Judy and I vote for chicken noodle and chicken noodle it is."

"Well, if it's chicken noodle, I like the Bouser better than the Angela's."

"Why? We've never had it at home."

"Because it looks good in the TV ad and the mother in the ad says it has more chicken than Angela's."

"We have always eaten Angela's. It's the oldest brand around and no one has complained about it."

"What about the store brand? I've had it and liked it a lot."

"I think it has monosodium glutamate in it, Dad, and that's not good for you."

"Who told you that, Paul?"

"I heard it on the radio the other day."

"Well, let's read the labels to check for monosodium glutamate and also see if we can learn which has the most chicken."

"The Angela's is the only one without it."

"OK, that leaves only one decision, how many cans can we eat tonight."

Nearly every parent can attest to the authenticity of this story. The principles herein apply to a very broad array of product buying decisions. For this reason I ask you to consider the following questions as a marketing person.

1. How many decisions were necessary in this buying process?
2. How many people could say no but not say yes and have it mean anything?
3. What marketing efforts came into play?
4. From which brand's Marketing Department?
5. Was there an influencer that none of the marketing departments were aware of?
6. What was the most effective marketing medium?
7. What role did the label play?
8. Was there a need for interaction between the buyer and the seller?
9. What role did interaction between buying committee members play?
10. Was the product simple or complex and did that affect the buying process?
11. How many people on the buying committee needed education?
12. How, and by whom was it delivered?
13. What was the perception of a difference of the Angela's brand?
14. What was the perception of a difference of the Bouser brand?
15. How was that POD created and made visible to the buying committee?
16. There was no mention of a shelf talker, but if one had been displayed with one of the soups being discussed, what would its effect have been?

Complex Buying Process, Simple Product

This was a complex buying process for a fairly simple product. Plain, unsalted, chicken broth would have been a simpler product. The complexity came from the number of people who would be affected by its purchase and "installation." These answers to the questions summarize the input of several groups that participated in this exercise.

- At least five decisions were necessary.

- The two parents could say no. Mom could say yes and make it stick. Dad could say no but only very diplomatically; his yes was helpful but not weighty.

- There were both marketing and negotiating efforts as in "let's have three kinds." The children were marketing on Dad's behalf by offering to take out the veggies they didn't like and he did, none of which would be in chicken noodle but would be in the vegetable beef. The Bouser TV ad must have been pretty direct in its comparison of chicken content to Angela's. Apparently Angela's had been relying on its reputation. The presence of monosodium glutamate was suddenly important because of a person talking on the radio. That person was the influencer. Only brands with that chemical in the ingredient list would be affected.

- First reaction is TV, but radio made an impact. I first thought it was safe to assume that none of the Marketing Departments involved were aware of the influencer on the radio: then Walt (my Editor) reminded me that one of the Marketing Departments may well have planted the story.

- The store brand label appears to be the only one listing a critical ingredient. That fact took the store's brand out of contention but also mandated that the competitor's labels be read.

- The label became the key to the complete education of the buyers after the potential harm from monosodium glutamate became known.

- The seller in this case is the soup manufacturer's Marketing Department. No human-to-human interaction between buyer and seller was needed to make a buying decision.

- The buying committee included everyone in the vehicle. Their interaction and cross selling resulted in a hassle-free dinner after everyone got to the table.

- The product is relatively simple, yet complex enough in terms of ingredients, to lengthen the buying process when compared to Mom going to the store alone.

- In essence everyone needed some level of education about two things: the amount of chicken in the mix and the presence or absence of monosodium glutamate.

- The original delivery of the education about content was the TV advertisement for the chicken and the radio for the other ingredient. The label on the can delivered key education; intermediate level education was delivered by members of the buying committee.

- Angela's perception of a difference includes dependability and satisfactory if not superior taste.

- Bouser was unknown to all but the committee member who had the perception that it had more chicken and therefore was superior.

- This perception of a difference was created by the TV ad and made visible by apparently the only member who had seen it.

Did you think the label wasn't important because buying a can of soup is simple?

Shelf Talkers

Question 16 isn't a trick question. It comes to mind for me, because some 30 years before this writing, a soup company ran an experiment with shelf talkers with fascinating results.

They created a shelf talker that simply said, "**Good Soup.**" When it was placed on the shelf below chicken noodle, sales of chicken noodle more than doubled for about two weeks. This effect disappeared in the third week. When the same shelf talker was then placed under a different soup, the effect for that soup was the same. It worked best if a week passed between different flavors of soup. The company stopped the use of such shelf talkers after a few years, perhaps because it seemed too simple to new people who joined the Marketing Department.

It still works because people have not changed. In the years since the soup company's experiment at least two research projects done by candidates for masters and doctoral degrees showed that between 55 and 60 percent of *all* purchases are the result of impulse or have impulse involved in them. Shelf talkers trigger impulse buying. Though I have not seen them used for this purpose, they could also reduce the frustration caused by another modern phenomenon.

Too Many Options

As originally used, the **Good Soup** shelf talker triggered impulse buying by bringing attention to a single selection out of many varieties of soup. It was thought that it primarily caught the attention of a buyer predisposed to buying soup; in reality it caused some soup purchases by people passing the soup display on their way to another product. Without the shelf talker these soup purchases would not have happened, because the number of soups available from the soup manufacturer that devised the shelf talker demanded a time consuming decision process.

On my second visit to Paris, France, I wanted some cheese to munch on with bread and wine in my hotel room. I walked a short distance to a cheese shop and came out over an hour later with two kinds of cheese. If I had limited myself to one kind it would have taken more than two hours. The reason was that France produces more than 450 different cheeses and this cheese shop had at least 200 on display. That was OK for me feeding myself but if my wife, who also likes cheese, had been with me we might still be in the store.

Modern marketers have created a real challenge for themselves by offering many options for simple necessities. Dishwasher soap comes in four scents and three package sizes and too often the economical large size costs more per ounce than the medium size. This bewilders, frustrates, and then angers you and me when we are short of time and tired. My favorite supermarket prints the cost per ounce on the shelf price tag. That makes package size selection easy; it does not help me decide which flavor of beans to buy before or after shoppers have mixed them up on the shelf.

In the story where I went to the store for milk and came home with several bottles of wine, the problem reared its ugly head. Each bottle I came home with was purchased because something made it stand out from the rest. Your challenge in marketing is to help me select from 20 kinds of

Merlot. I guarantee that putting shelf talkers under every different variety on the shelf is not the answer. A shelf talker that says Preferred Selection might prove useful. You will need to be careful in its use, however, lest it earn the same fate as Vintners Reserve on a wine. At one time those words on the label truly designated a top rated bottle from a single winery. When other wineries copied this approach it worked until one of them added these words to labels on its least desirable wines. Even the inexperienced consumer could discern the difference. It proved to be a costly marketing error.

The problem is not confined to grocery shopping. Too many options can destroy sales on the Internet just as easily.

> My wife received a gift certificate issued by a major seller on the Internet. The certificate plainly stated that it could be used for any product she found after entering the seller's website. She discovered a vast array of products through various links and found exactly what she wanted in one location. She decided to look at a couple of other possibilities but could not find her way back to the one she really wanted: after two hours she gave up and purchased nothing. She may never use the gift certificate.

This is not an isolated case. Two weeks later she made the decision to begin paying a credit card issued by our bank using the on-line pay service, by transferring funds from a checking account to the credit card account with the same bank. Twenty-five minutes later she completed the set up. Two hours later she received confirmation and learned that a $6.95 monthly fee would be charged. This being unacceptable she could not find a way to cancel the service without going to a bank branch in person. She believes this is sheer stupidity.

I believe it is a case of incomplete education about a product by the bank's Marketing Department. Incomplete education of the customer as a result of incomplete education of the application software programmers that created the website, followed by incomplete follow up on the part of the Marketing Department.

In developing your Marketing Plan, ask yourself:

- Is this product unique?

- If so, what do I need to provide in education to the prospective buyer?

- If it isn't unique, what must I do to make it stand out from all the other options and make it easy to decide to select and buy it.

Think About Your Product Before You Write The Marketing Plan

Now, think about the product you are selling or are considering selling and ask yourself, "Is it a complex product or is its use complex?"

A bottle of red wine contains over 400 chemical components and requires more than a year to produce, but you only need to unscrew the cap or pull the cork to use it. It is a complex product, but very simple to use. Neither the complexity of the wine nor the simplicity of opening the bottle and drinking it will affect the average buyer's buying process.

A mowing and landscape planting and maintenance service is a complex product that is simpler to use than the bottle of wine because you just watch the work being done. The product's complexity of use will most affect the buying process, not the complexity of the product per se. The more complex the product's use, the more education that will be needed for each individual involved in the buying process.

The buying process for a bottle of wine can range in complexity from the low level in the hermit's purchase of a can of beans to the much higher level in the soup for dinner story. The number of people who will share the bottle, the buyer's knowledge of their individual levels of wine knowledge, and the foods that will accompany the wine will all affect the buying process. The chemical complexity of the typical red wine will have little effect on the complexity of the buying process.

The landscape service will be a very complex buying process for several reasons illustrated in this true story. Again, note what makes the process complex.

I Watched You Drive By Without Stopping, What Happened?

Our home sat on a one-acre lot on the perimeter of a golf course. Our four children and I had laboriously hand-planted the back and side areas with plugs of grass sod. We also planted a 15-foot deep strip in between the front of the house and the driveway. We lived in the desert and decided to leave the rest of the lot in its natural condition with no water other than the scant normal rainfall.

In the two years it took for the grass plugs to spread out and give us a nice lawn, we planted some trees and shrubs and learned how to trim and care for them. The older children and I shared the weekly task of mowing the grass and I kept the shrubs trimmed. The grass area was beautiful and for two years the natural desert front yard was quite acceptable. Then we experienced some years with above normal rainfall. The grass area thrived and so did the desert front yard. It became a graphic demonstration of how the seeds of desert plants survive for years and come to life when *enough* rain falls. Those wild flowers became a two-to-three foot high jungle. My work had come to include almost weekly travel and two of the children had moved out to college. It was time to bite the bullet and purchase a mowing and landscape service.

What steps in the buying process had we completed at this point?

Steps one and two: We had perceived a want and converted it to a need.

We studied the business directory pages and made phone calls. The responses we received on the phone were real lessons in the power of the perception of a difference. Between tone of voice, words spoken with a mouthful of chewing gum, accents that made understanding very difficult, and just lack of courtesy, we ended up with a very small list of possibilities. We drove the streets stopping to look at homes where landscape services were at work and looked at the results. All of this was part of our self-education about landscape maintenance service.

We had received estimates on the phone but no details in writing. The quotes all seemed high in relation to our confidence in what the results would be. When Amy suggested I call a dear and wealthy friend for a recommendation, I balked on the grounds that anyone he would recommend would be too expensive for us. She insisted, I called, and he convinced me I should call the service that kept their place looking so nice.

Johnny spoke English and Spanish clearly, with good sentence structure. His vehicle was clean, obviously well cared for. He was well groomed and wore a work outfit befitting his business. My level of confidence grew from the time I first saw him. Amy liked him from the beginning of his visit, and so did the two children still at home. He had a great perception of a difference. As we walked the property he educated us about his service, as it would apply to our specific situation. We had started our walk in the front and worked our way around the house. Now we stood facing that desert jungle.

"I will clean everything up so it looks the way you would make it look if you had the time and I will keep it looking that way on a weekly basis. I will keep the flowerbeds weeded and clean and replant them in spring and fall. You can stop my services at any time. I want to be paid in advance on the first visit each month with cash or check. I will make you glad Mr. Ed recommended me. I will start on Monday. The price will be $1,600 for the first cleanup and $150 each month after that."

The price rocked me, but the front was a mess and I liked this man. He had made no effort to push me into a decision, he had answered all my questions, even those I had not asked. I looked at Amy and she signaled her approval. I wrote a check, handed it to him, and we shook hands. We were at ease with the decision because he had completed the education we needed to be able to make a decision. His last comment was,

"You won't recognize the place."

The next day, Sunday, I flew to the east coast. I returned in a taxi at dusk on Friday evening. I instructed the driver on how to get to our home and leaned back to rest.

"Are we on the right street?"

"Yes, I'll tell you when we get to my house."

"This is Hayden, I thought you said it was before we reached Hayden?"

"It is. Turn around and drive slowly, it will be on the right side of the street."

"Are you sure you've been here before?"

Amy was waiting in front of the house when we pulled in.

"I watched you drive by without stopping. What happened?"

"I didn't recognize the place!"

When I surveyed the scene early the next morning, the price of $1,600 no longer rocked me, I thought it was low! When we started the buying process, Amy and I came to the conclusion that we might be able to handle $800 for the first clean up and $110 a month. I knew that the mowing would take eight hours a month, which if it was all a service would do, was a good hourly figure at the time. I expected to do all other work myself. The education process did not cause us to discuss a change in those cost expectations, but it did subliminally change our perception of what we'd like if we could afford it.

Our education came from several sources over a period of weeks.

- The business directory advertisements told us the breadth of available services. This is where we learned we could select lawn mowing only or a raft of additional things. The directory also yielded the names of providers located in our area of the city and suburbs and how long some of them had been in business. Stability and staying power were indicators of satisfied customers to us.

- We learned, through observation of many homes, that formal clipped and shaped shrubs did not fit our personalities. We liked freedom of expression combined with neatness. We are warm, expressive people and landscaping that allows plants to show their natural form fits us. It turned out that not many landscape maintenance people have the skills to do this when trimming plants and shrubs.

- People doing landscape maintenance educated us without knowing it. We looked for their vehicles on the streets as we drove, observed the condition of the vehicles themselves, the appearance of the workers, and results of their efforts as viewed from the street.

- We compared what we saw on the streets with the way we were treated on the phone when we called these providers and found that good looking vehicles could not overcome the perceptions that formed when we were making phone calls. It was fascinating.

- Our friend provided education when we called for his recommendation. He had used two other providers before connecting with Johnny, and told us what the differences were. He talked about consistency of service, completeness of service, and willingness to conform to his and his wife's desires and idiosyncrasies. Everything he talked about had to do with the actions of people. He did not talk about vehicles, equipment, or the appearance of people. He did not create a visual perception of Johnny and his people.

Johnny completed our education. The perception that formed in my mind, in that crucial first 30 seconds, fit perfectly with the kind of person our friend had described. This was a man of substance who liked his people, his work, and was successful in it. His comments as we walked the property indicated that he looked at the situation as a whole, while seeing the details that make the difference in the whole. He was quietly confident and that built my confidence in him. He created a strong perception of a difference and indeed he made a difference in our lives for years.

Packaging A Service Product

Much of the preceding discussion has dealt with tangible products, e.g., beans, soup. We are accustomed to using the package to educate ourselves about the product. Services present a different packaging challenge.

Please go back and read the last story again while looking for the effect of good and bad packaging in our buying decision process. The landscaping services packaging was their vehicles and the people doing the work. The condition of vehicles, e.g., rust spots, bent fenders, and readability of the identifying signage educated us about their business acumen and stability. Mowers and tools that were encrusted with dried grass educated us as to their pride and workmanship.

People that wore full uniforms or shirts and caps bearing the company name were more desirable to us than those without; however, dirty uniforms, etc., were far less desirable than clean clothes that were not uniforms. Johnny's truck was clean and shiny though not brand new. His work uniform did not have a printed message but it was clean and pressed. When his people came on site they did not wear uniforms but they were well groomed every day. Their equipment was obviously hosed off and cleaned at the end of every day. This was packaging that educated.

Note that the people (what they did and what they said on the phone and in person) were an integral part of the packaging. They could negate everything else that we had heard in the first few seconds of a telephone conversation. The way they went about their work educated us about their relationship with their supervisor and company. Their finished work completed the packaging.

Now all you have to do is apply these principles to the marketing plan for your product — the one you are charged with bringing to a profitable level of sales. The answers to the 27 questions contain all the raw material you need. Study those answers, then build a plan for the education of the buyer and everyone who will provide that education, while creating a perception of a desirable difference.

Let's look at an example from the past. Since we were not present when this product came into being, we will answer the questions using some literary license.

Chapter 4

An Example From The Past

The easiest way to see the breadth as well as the gross detail of Marketing in a company is by

seeing an example. After pondering this for some time I chose a company that has survived for

over a century. The strength and consistency of its marketing has enabled it to live through several

severe setbacks. I have read several histories of its life, used its products, and observed it for

many years. With that background, my experience in Marketing and Sales, and my imagination,

I present this reconstruction of what must have happened to keep it successful.

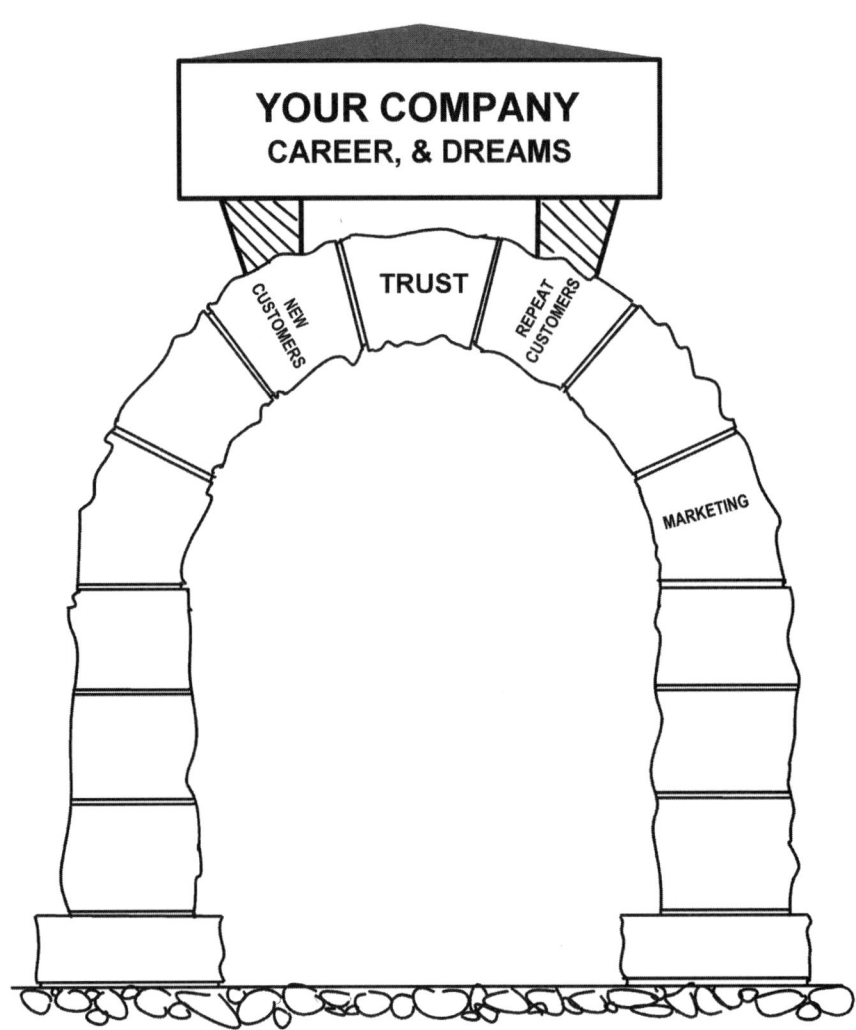

YOUR COMPANY
CAREER, & DREAMS

NEW CUSTOMERS

TRUST

REPEAT CUSTOMERS

MARKETING

The Business Arch

A Century-Long Marketing Challenge

Horses and bicycles were the main methods of personal transportation before the advent of the automobile. Until Henry Ford began producing the Model T, early autos were expensive and did not make much of a dent in the use of bicycles. Bicycles were slow, but they were fun to ride. The solution was the addition of a small gasoline engine to a bicycle. The resulting motorcycles filled the need for faster transportation at a cost far below that of early automobiles. Entrepreneurs in many parts of the world filled that need.

Imagine yourself as the newly hired Marketing Department person asking the 27 questions of Mr. Harley and Mr. Davidson as they show you the second motorcycle to be designed and built in America. The year is 1903.

1. How soon will new technology make this product obsolete or unnecessary?

    Not in the foreseeable future.

2. How soon can production quantities be on the shipping dock?

    Two months.

3. What must the buyer do to install and use this product?

    Learn to ride a bicycle and send us an order with a check for payment in full. Uncrate the cycle, read the instructions, install the handlebars in the correct position for personal comfort, fill the tank with gas, reread the instructions, and start the engine.

4. What will this cost the buyer in addition to the purchase price?

   The shipping cost and gasoline cost.

5. What does this product do?

   It carries the rider anywhere a bicycle will go with the same ease of handling, at speeds up to 15 miles an hour.

6. What does this do for the buyer?

   You can be independent: go where you wish, when you wish, explore new places, feel the wind in your face, and the power of the engine under you.

7. Of what value is this to the buyer?

   It's fun, brother!

8. What percentage of this value is quantifiable, how much is perceived?

   In reality it is all perceived; however, each buyer will find a way to justify the price after taking a trial ride.

9. What does the buyer do or use to obtain this value currently?

   Rides a bicycle or buys an automobile and puts the top and windshield down.

10. Is this clearly a better way or just an alternate choice among many?

It is clearly a better way with almost no restrictions on where you can go.

11. If clearly a better or totally new way, how quickly will competitors appear?

Competitors are already here. European makes are about to be imported and the Indian Motorcycle Company is building motorcycles in this country.

12. If an alternate choice, why should it be perceived as preferable?

It is better engineered and longer lasting because we have designed it to function well on dirt and gravel roads. It is easy to ride.

13. What is the expected usable life of this product?

If serviced properly it should have the same useful life as a good bicycle.

14. Will the buyer need or want a replacement when it wears out?

Yes, because the fun will not be outgrown.

15. Is it important that the product be durable, or just maintainable?

It must be durable enough to be worry-free and easily maintainable for low cost of ownership. For many owners this will be a primary form of transportation to and from work when weather and road conditions permit.

16. What will it cost to put the product on the shipping dock?

This is yet to be determined because it is a function of volume. We have built two and determined the tooling that is needed to make the task easier. We will provide costs within a month.

At this point you have asked Mr. Harley and Mr. Davidson the questions they can answer easily. The answers to the following questions are your responsibility as the person writing the Product Marketing Plan.

17. How many potential buyers exist?

*In 1903, when these questions could have been asked, modern statistics did not exist. As the person in charge of Marketing, you would probably have taken a ride on the cycle and discovered just how great the wind in your hair and power between your legs felt. After that you would have made a scientific wild ass guess (**S.W.A.G.**) which would at least have been greater than the first two years production capability. Today you will use a computer with communication to the world's data banks and learn within moments all you need to know to answer this and the next question.*

18. Where are they located, in what density in each location?

In all major cities, as well as larger towns. In small towns and villages gasoline is not readily available. This will change with time.

19. How do these buyers usually learn about the existence of a product like this?

They read the local newspapers, both articles and advertisements. They talk with owners they see riding around.

20. What will it cost to make them aware of its existence?

The cost to send articles to newspapers about this new, useful, fun-to-ride form of cycle and to print and distribute picture posters and descriptions to every bicycle shop in each town.

21. What will the buyer need to learn during the buying process?

The fact that riding the motorcycle is similar to but more fun than riding a bicycle because you give it more gas to speed up, which is much easier than pedaling furiously. The size and seat height are the same as a bicycle. Maintaining the machine regularly is quite similar to a bicycle except for the motor, which should have major work done by a trained mechanic.

22. How will this information be delivered to the buyer and the mechanic?

It is possible that all of it can be delivered via printed instructions. The buyer should have instructions for maintaining those items that don't require great expertise or skill. These can be in an Operator's Manual. Instructions for the mechanic should include sketches, engineering blueprints, and "cut-away view" illustrations. The mechanic should have hands-on training and be equipped with any special tools we have developed for use in the factory. This would be the least expensive approach.

Another approach is to sell selected bicycle store operators on the idea of augmenting their business by selling our motorcycle as an additional product line. One or more of their service people could come to our training school and provide additional income to the store operator by servicing our motorcycles.

23. Who will do the educating?

Marketing will prepare the printed materials and instruction sheets. The Engineering Department will prepare diagrams and "cut-away view" illustrations. Marketing will design the mechanic's training course and materials. Marketing will prepare proposed standards for the selection of bicycle store operators and the conditions and rules, which will govern their relationship with us. Management and Legal will convert these into proper contractual documents. A factory salesperson will be appointed by management to implement the selection of store operators. Marketing will provide the product training needed by the salesperson and support him as needed. Marketing will not teach the salesperson how to sell. Marketing will research with users, trial ride the Indian motorcycle, and prepare information comparing it to our cycle for use by the factory salesperson.

24. What will be the delivered cost of the buyer's education?

Marketing will develop this on a cost per first year, cost per second year, and cost per motorcycle delivered in each year basis, with help and advice from Accounting.

25. What price to the buyer will make the product profitable to all involved?

Marketing will be responsible for setting this price. It will do so after Accounting has produced direct and indirect cost to manufacture and package for shipment. Marketing will work with Accounting in determining distribution, marketing, and selling costs.

26. Why will the buyer be willing to pay this price?

Marketing will do an analysis of the capabilities of existing competing products and talk with users of them. The conversations will be structured so as to cause the user of a competing product to expound on why they use the product, the needs or wants that it satisfies, and its strengths and weaknesses in comparison to them. This will provide assurance that our motorcycle will indeed be competitive at the price marketing sets.

27. When, after product introduction, will price be primary in the buying decision?

This cannot be determined at this time with a product concept so new. It is Marketing's ongoing responsibility to forecast when price will become primary and adjust it up or down as needed to keep our motorcycle competitive, desirable, and profitable in the market place.

With these answers in hand, (continuing to imagine you are in charge of marketing for this product), do you consider this to be much of a marketing challenge?

If yes, why? If no, why not?

What kind of research and 'what if' thinking would you do today to predict when it could become a challenge?

Could you write a Marketing Plan for this product now?

You should say, "Yes."

You should say yes because you have all the information you need.

✧✧✧

For more than 100 years, this product has been competitive against other motorcycles, desirable in the market, and the producer has been profitable. The first years were relatively easy. To be sure, you, as head of marketing for the company, were very busy.

You set up the training courses, trained the people that became the sales department, designed the materials they needed to recruit the dealers, and taught them how to educate people interested in buying motorcycles. Your descriptive literature stressed mechanical attributes and dependability because this matched the culture of that period.

You were selling an alternate form of daily transportation, the price of which was so far below that for an automobile you didn't bother to stress it in the literature. However, when automobiles became cheaper to buy and usable in any weather, the marketing of motorcycles became a challenge. Now the majority of owners considered them a toy, not a necessity.

You started doing some research and discovered that people who had motorcycles did not give them up easily when times were tough and money was tight. The culture of the day was cash; credit cards didn't exist and time payments were used sparingly. Therefore, the motorcycle was invariably paid for so the only cost of continued ownership was gas, oil, tires, and replacement parts. This was good because you did not have to compete with used cycles when selling new ones, but people weren't buying new toys.

At this point you went back in the files and looked at the questions Mr. Harley and Mr. Davidson had answered years before. You really thought about their answers to questions five through eight and 14. You rode a motorcycle yourself and many of your friends did, so you asked them these questions and checked their answers against your own feelings. The answers had not changed much over the years. The culture and the market for transportation had changed but these questions had nothing to do with these factors. They had everything to do with human curiosity and emotional satisfaction. You went to sleep one night thinking about this and in the morning you wrote these words.

"Harley-Davidson. Makes every path a highway."

You put this on the bottom of a picture depicting a man riding a Harley-Davidson motorcycle on a path alongside a river. He is passing a boy wearing a straw hat, sitting on the riverbank fishing with a cane pole.

You put this picture with no other words, nothing else, in newspapers, magazines, on posters, on the back of playing cards, and on square throw pillows which attracted attention laying on the sofa in the living room.* You, the person in charge of marketing for Harley-Davidson, sold a lot of motorcycles with it.

It Worked

It worked because it was simple.

It worked because it told a story.

It worked because it allowed us to think about it and fill in our words, our longings.

It worked for over one hundred years because its simple story was repeated for each new generation of customers without being allowed to degenerate into a torrent of useless words.

I was not yet born when that ad was conceived and I did not see it until I was given a re-creation of the pillow when I began dreaming and saving for my third Harley after many, many years of driving big, solid, safe automobiles. Those autos gave me independence, and two of them, soft-top convertibles, gave me the wind in my hair, but they didn't provide the feeling of adventure that a motorcycle had. I even drove one convertible to and from work for 12 months without ever putting the top up in an attempt to re-create the feelings and emotions of riding a cycle.

---

*My children gave me a re-creation of the pillow some years ago. It has a place of honor in my bedroom.

The picture in the original advertisement was out-of-date the moment the company produced improved motorcycles that looked different. Rerunning the ad with a new model cycle wouldn't have worked because clothing styles changed and the pace of our culture had speeded up so much that even ten-year-old boys didn't want to sit on a riverbank, fishing with a cane pole. The modern marketing approach is to produce a media spot filled with a torrent of words and shots of motorcycles with very loud exhaust pipes, doing things no sane person would consider doing, followed with a five-second chance to read a disclaimer saying that what you see was done by professional drivers on a section of highway closed for the purpose.*

Those old time marketing people did it differently. They created a monthly publication, which today would be called a newsletter or magazine. It was black on white glossy paper, not over 16 pages as I recall, and it sold on a subscription basis.

Eleven months of the year it had stories and pictures about trips that people had taken riding the company's cycles. The pictures were taken and contributed by the ordinary people that had taken the trip; at least this was the perception this reader had. Certainly the photography, poses, and costumes were not professional. They showed the adventure of riding through the forests of northern Minnesota and Wisconsin, the farm land of Iowa, the colored leaves of autumn in Ohio, and the northeast. It made my mouth water. It said everything the original ad had said. It said it eloquently because *it let me create the words in my mind*. It carried the theme, year after year, consistently saying, "It's fun, brother."

---

*I've made this sentence long to demonstrate the effect modern media advertising spots have on a potential customer. To really get a feel for it, try reading it out loud, really fast!

Every issue included news of motorcycle club events around the country. Racing was a part of the culture of the day and the success of racers riding the company's cycles was duly recorded. Safe driving tips were always present as were advertisements for cycle accessories and clothing made by or licensed by the company. Once a year the new models were shown with detailed stories on mechanical improvements. This publication was not free to the owner of the company's motorcycle, as was the case later. Nonetheless, it found its way into barbershop reading racks and many other places where younger men would see it.

When the company came out with different size and horsepower models, women joined the customer ranks. Their pictures and stories appeared in it. Its message and the method of communicating did not change. It educated the reader about the fun and independence of riding a motorcycle. It educated the buyer about the company's cycles and why they were very good. It never used the word "best," but it did convey dependability with sentences like, 'the entire 2000 miles were trouble free. We did nothing more than check air pressure and oil every morning.'

The theme was consistent, the message was simple, and *that is the secret of effective marketing*.

Marketing Can't Do It Alone

Marketing…

- Created the dealer selection policies.

- Guided the creation of instruction books for dealer mechanics, now called technicians.

- Learned about competitor's cycles, created comparisons of strengths and weaknesses of competitors and the company's cycles, and included them in product training classes for the salespeople.

- Marketing did not teach the salespeople how to sell, but it supported them with everything they needed to teach the dealer's team how to educate the person making the buying decision.

- Marketing provided Sales with sales collaterals, including brochures, posters, and engineering white papers. These explained how and why the cycles and engines were being changed over the years to ensure dependability and serviceability.

- Above all else, Marketing talked and listened to the salespeople.

- Marketing also kept potential buyers aware of the company name and product, though it allowed the product's presence on the streets and roadways to do most of that.

Everyone in marketing rode a motorcycle and spent time with motorcycle owners. They listened to the salespeople explaining the dealer's problems and listened to the motorcyclists they rode with. This gave them great insight into what needed to be changed on the current models and what should be kept. They shared this insight and knowledge with the design engineers and manufacturing people, who either listened or heard it repeated so often they had to accept it.

The result was a solid, consistently dependable product that seemed to evolve, instead of jumping from one plateau to another when forced to by competition. This consistency created trust and earned great loyalty from customers, enabling the company to survive depressions and all manner of recessions, with a product that over the years became a recreational tool seldom used for "useful work."

The message here is loud and clear. Marketing was important as a member of and sometimes the glue that held a team together. Everyone on that team was involved in Customer Care, not just Marketing or Sales. Everyone on that team added to the desirable difference that cycle owners and others perceived when they came into contact with the company, its dealers, and its products. That perception of a difference was the power that carried the company through more than a century of providing satisfaction for its employees, suppliers, dealers, and customers.

The Perception Of A Difference Is Fragile

That wonderful perception of a difference disappeared when the privately owned company was sold to a large corporation, whose modern management wanted faster growth and greater profit margins. It occurred during the era when cutting costs everywhere, including every step of manufacture, was considered the way to boost profits quickly. Based on observed results, the application of this philosophy to a manufacturing team, in which every member took individual responsibility for quality and craftsmanship, went over like a lead balloon.

It may have been the new philosophy or lessened attention to detail by individuals throughout the company, but in any event, the quality of the company's cycles degraded rapidly. The air-cooled engines required precise tolerances that allowed for wide variations in temperature to enable dependable operation in snowy cold and extreme desert heat. This had never been a problem for the rider before the change in company ownership; now it was. Cycles were being returned with parts that had frozen at highway speeds, shortly after the factory-prescribed break-in procedure and well within the warranty period. News of these failures spread through the customer base like wildfire in a dry forest. Customers either kept their old cycle or turned to the competition. The perception of a difference turned negative and trust died.

Rather than see their old company fail and destroy the dreams of all the people that had made it a part of the world community, some of the original principals successfully regained control. It took a while, but the perception of a difference was restored, the team spirit reactivated, quality returned, and the company went on to become one of the few that have lasted for more than a century. The story of this company is the story of the power of the perception of a difference. It is also a powerful example of the negative effect "management" can create and the positive effect of "leadership" on the perception of a difference and its power.

What have you learned about marketing from this story?

I learned that… (Write what you learned.)

How did marketing make the buying process easy and satisfying?

Except for the period under unwise management this company had very few cases of buyer's remorse. What do you think produced this result?

Were We Correct?

When we began the discussion about marketing plans, were we correct in saying that the first item in the finished marketing plan would be making the buyer aware of the product's existence?

Considering all the tasks that had to be done in the case of the motorcycle, would it be wiser to set up the training courses and write the instruction manuals before starting the buyer awareness (advertising) program?

I have witnessed the chaos that results when the number of buyers greatly exceeds the ability and capacity to deliver the education buyers need when the production team blindly ships product to everyone who orders. The people in Customer Care went crazy. It was akin to shipping a complex unassembled product without including the assembly instructions in the box and when people start calling up, discovering that assembly instructions don't exist.

In reading the history of the motorcycle company, as written by many authors, it is apparent that sales took off slowly enough to enable all of the supporting steps to be executed in time to prevent buyer's remorse. It's also apparent that marketing people constantly revised, rewrote, and retrained as a result of listening to customers and owning a motorcycle themselves.

The lesson is clear: If you are marketing canned beans, go to the store late in the day, decide which flavor you want, and pay attention to how the selection decision was made. After eating it, decide how well the label describes the beans. Eating them in the company test kitchen will not give you the same insights. One company CEO went to his local supermarket and observed people educating themselves about the plastic food storage containers his company was proudly selling, because they were "easy to close and open." The next morning he told the engineers who had conceived and designed the product to change the design so a woman could open the "easy to close and open" container without breaking her fingernails. (That turned out to be quite a challenge.)

On learning about this I asked myself why didn't someone in Marketing do this observing? It should not have been the CEO, though his doing it was heralded as an example of his astuteness. It was Marketing's job and it should have been done before the product was approved for production.

As I said at the beginning, this story is a mix of observed fact and imagination. The motorcycle company is real. I am enjoying their re-creation of my second cycle at present. The marketing, training, education, and advertising really happened. That is why they exist today.

The story is my effort to show you the real responsibility of Marketing in a real company. It describes what I would expect the Marketing organization to do in any company I founded or became CEO of. I currently serve on the Board of a small company that performs all of these functions with great success. The functions are performed by several members of management as part of their daily responsibility. They don't think of it as marketing and may not realize it until they read this book. When they do they will learn why they survived and grew in a very tough market, for more than 30 years. It is my sincere hope that you experience the same success.

Looking Forward

You begin a Product Marketing Plan at the end point, the final step in making people aware of the product's existence, and work back to the beginning. This task is the one most of us think is the most important thing Marketing does. Now that you know this isn't true, let's talk about awareness creation.

Chapter 5

Creating Awareness

Now that you know what Marketing really does, it is time to discuss what many people

think is the *only* thing it does. Creating awareness is a vital part of Marketing's charter.

When done well at the correct time it ensures the success of the product.

Correct timing creates awareness when the product is available to be seen, touched,

and used by the buyer and not before. This is the most critical timing issue. A secondary issue

is timing in relation to the market's ability to absorb the product at the rate the seller

desires without creating demand that outruns the seller's productive capacity.

Creating awareness requires communication that is clear, understandable, and memorable.

The message is important, but without these key elements nobody will hear it and

the product will die for want of buyers.

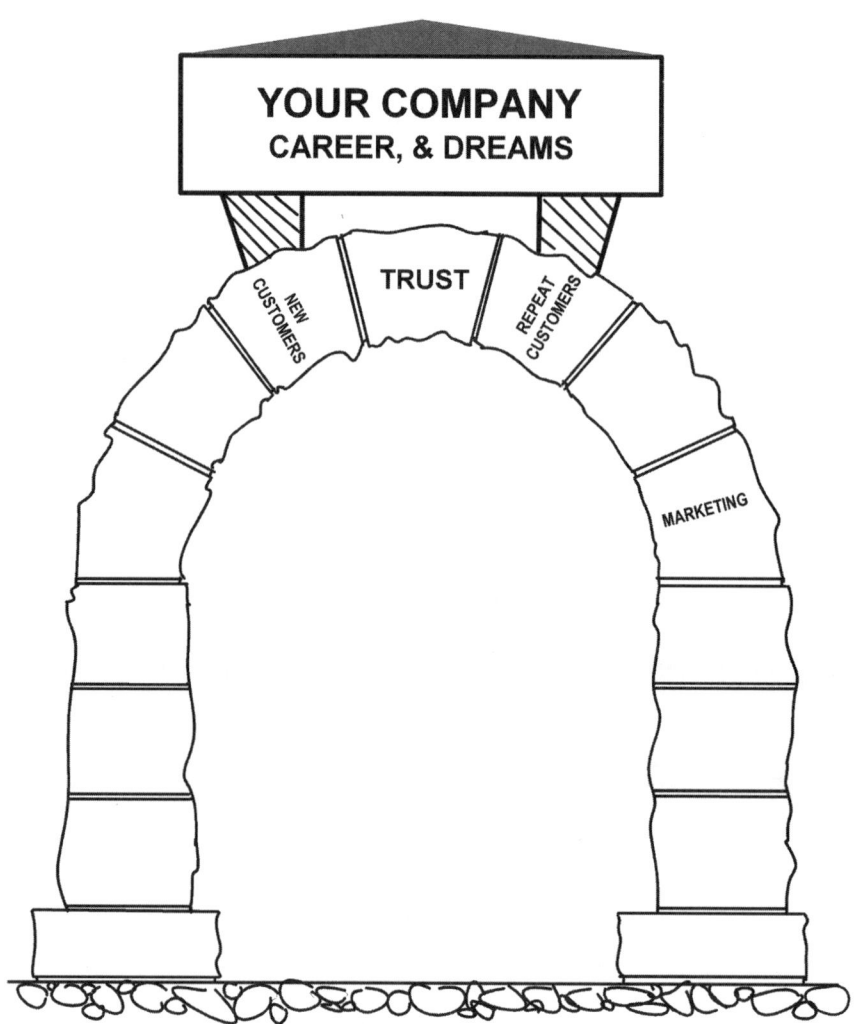

The Business Arch

Creating awareness cost effectively should be the goal of Marketing. It is easily accomplished if Marketing is involved with a product from its inception, because the needed research is part of the whole process. When Marketing is not involved from the beginning there is no time for complete research. The result is truckloads of money wasted on advertising that does not reach the minds of potential buyers because it uses the wrong media or the correct media in the wrong way.

The salesperson is probably the oldest awareness-creation method. Gutenberg's invention of movable type made print awareness creation cost effective. Direct mail was a personalized form of print. Radio was its first real competitor, then the movies followed by television, and after a short breather the Web and e-mail, which will soon be followed with new technology. Since each new method has not replaced an earlier one, the difficulty of choosing the most cost effective method becomes staggering.

You've seen how the motorcycle company created and maintained awareness very cost effectively. The stories in this chapter show how some marketing people have addressed the task. Their successes and failures will give you ideas and some laughs. Please enjoy and apply what they tell you as appropriate to your challenge.

Let's Talk About Advertising

The basic purpose of advertising is to make me, the potential buyer, aware that a product exists and cause me to want to know more about the results of its use in my situation. Your advertising must address these four facts:

1. I cannot buy from you until I know you exist.

2. I cannot buy a product from you until I know you sell/carry it.

3. I cannot buy a product until I know its purpose.

4. I cannot buy a product until I know the results of its use and how they will benefit me.

Until I know these things, the price of the product and how it compares to similar products is unimportant and totally irrelevant to me. *I don't need or want to know everything the first time you contact me about a product.* Your ad, the first time I see or hear it, will be your first contact with me. Remember also that price is not very important in my buying decision. Think carefully about this when you begin planning advertising for your next product.

We Put A Sign In The Window

My brother and I operated a large hardware store in a medium size city at the time when television first became available in our area. We debated about selling television sets and decided against it. We reasoned that we could fill a greater need for our customers by being able to repair and adjust television sets. We talked it over with our employees and selected one who would learn enough to be able to repair all the brands sold in our area. We sent him through all the training schools, became certified by manufacturers, and purchased all needed equipment. We then put a sign in the window that simply said,

We repair TV sets; all makes, all models.

We designed a small, one column box ad that repeated this message and gave our name, address, and phone number. We placed this ad in the Sports section of both local newspapers and arranged for it to appear, on the same page and location on the page, in every issue week after week. It was not very costly and we treated it as an investment in our future. After two months we began to see some business that might have come to us because of the ad. In seven months, we realized that we needed to train another person.

We made the same investment in him as we had in the first person. We did this rather than have our first TV repair person train him for a couple of reasons. We did not want the first person to pass on any poor practices he might have developed. Also, in the formal classes the new person would learn the latest techniques. It was a good decision because he taught the first employee the new techniques.

Two years after we started running the ad, we had five people very busy repairing TV sets. We decided to limit the business to what five people could handle so the quality of our service could be maintained. We kept sending them to training schools whenever needed to keep up with product changes. We paid them top dollar and priced their services to make a profit for us. They earned the reputation of being the very best in the city. We **never changed the ad.** Best investment we ever made. We stayed in the TV repair business until new technology made them so reliable that replacement was better than repair.

We were our own Marketing Department. Looking back I realize that we made five marketing decisions that worked. With hindsight I now know why they worked.

1. We trained our people in advance so they could service all makes, all models. This was a marketing decision because it ensured that the first customer would be satisfied enough to tell friends about the service. Every succeeding customer did the same.

2. We continued to train new people and retrain the earlier ones so that every customer who came in four years after they started, went out satisfied enough to tell their friends about them. This was a strategic marketing decision.

3. We paid our technicians top dollar so they would not be tempted to go elsewhere and in the process we became the employer of choice in our area for this specialty. This was a marketing decision because people like and value consistency almost more than anything else.

4. We priced the service to make a profit after paying all the costs of training and advertising, knowing this made us the high priced service in our market area. This was a marketing decision, because you and I instinctively believe that we get what we pay for and always gravitate to the high priced product.

5. Our approach to advertising worked. It worked because it was simple, direct, and not confusing. It was easily stored in memory and easily recalled when your TV failed or a coworker commented that his/her TV had failed the evening before. It worked because when these situations arose, even if you didn't remember the ad copy, you did remember that it was in the Sports section and you often remembered what page in the Sports section. Because it was in every issue, you did

not have to look for an old issue or the Sunday issue; you just looked at today's paper. The ad copy made you aware of the existence of the business, the product (We repair TV sets; all makes, and models) and where the business was located. The ad copy and the decision to place it in the Sports section and have it on the same page in that section *in every issue of both papers,* was a marketing decision.

Five marketing decisions that worked:

Did you think of them as marketing decisions?

We didn't—to us they were just common sense good business. We did it because we wanted to succeed but not too fast and as cheaply as possible.

✧✧✧

If you are in marketing you will want to remember these decisions. Sell them to your superiors when they do not want to spend the money for training and compensation plans that will keep people in place.

Ask them if they feel more comfortable when they see the same faces in places they do business with every time they go there.

Ask them why they ask for the same captain and server in their favorite restaurant.

If they say they never thought about it, point out that it makes them more comfortable. Tell them you want to make your company's customers feel more comfortable and more inclined to do business with your company than with the competition.

Keeping the same people in place is marketing with the perception of a difference because people make the difference.

You may find it easier to sell this concept when you point out that it will enable your company to charge higher prices, make better profits, and increase customer satisfaction at the same time. Don't forget to tell them that an advertising agency may not be needed to write *simple, direct, honest* ad copy that people can understand.

KISMIF

Keep It Simple Make It Fun applies to marketing and especially to advertising. In the days when most men and a few women smoked, a common result was yellow front teeth. One brand of toothpaste was advertised on the radio with a simple lyric sung to a catchy, easy to remember tune.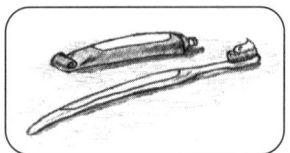

"You'll wonder where the yellow went when you brush your teeth with Pepsodent."

People hummed, whistled, and (in private) sang it. It sold a lot of toothpaste.

It was a short, cheap to buy, radio spot. It was simple and fun and it educated the buyer who smoked … and a lot of people who didn't.

I've lost count of the number of musical ads on radio that I and most other listeners could not understand. Ads in which the words were slurred, covered up by drum rolls, trumpet blasts, and other effects that made it impossible to know what was being sold and who was selling it. One was so bad and remained on radio long enough, that it became a subject of conversation when you met someone, 'did you figure out what that ad says?' No one we knew ever did.

Recently, I met with a person who promotes my seminar presentations. The first thing he asked when we sat down was,

"Have you seen that TV spot that shows all the green scenery and ends with the white haired man and little boy walking?"

"Yes, Amy and I saw it twice in Denver last week. What is it selling and who is selling it?"

"I don't know. I was hoping you could tell me. It is beautiful scenery that would be wonderful to visit but I don't know where it is located."

"I take it you don't advertise my work that way."

"For heavens sake, no! I tell people what the results will be from using you as a speaker and point out that there are no walkouts during your presentations. Then I tell them how to contact me to get you on their program."

This man is very creative and observant. He does a great job of promoting the people he represents yet he could not catch the meaning and purpose of this ad. I have not seen it since, but if it does come into view I will quickly close my eyes and listen to the words that must be spoken with it in an effort to find out what is being sold by whom.

Let My Mind Do The Work

TV advertising communicates through both my ears and my eyes. Radio uses my ears and my mind's eye, my imagination. "You'll wonder where the yellow went when you brush your teeth with Pepsodent" caused me to want to look in the mirror at my own teeth and it made me look at the teeth of other people to see if they were yellow. My mind made the ad very effective.

The same ad using TV might show a person with a toothy smile and teeth slightly touched up with yellow. This followed by the person brushing their teeth, and then by another toothy smile with the yellow all gone. Oh, of course, the toothpaste package would be lying on the sink with Pepsodent sharply focused. The white tooth smile would be directed at a man whose back would be toward camera. A voice would be extolling the virtues of using the product, which is what many ads do. In reality, in this case, the only words needed would be "You'll wonder where the yellow went, when you brush your teeth with Pepsodent" sung to that catchy tune during the last scene with the now white tooth smile directed at the man with his back to us. Simplicity sells because it lets us, the viewer, add the words that work for us.

Of course it will be a woman brushing her teeth because of the myth that sex sells… it doesn't. It just gets the attention of the viewer. The message and whether I remember it is what counts. If I insert my own words, in my mind, I will remember it far longer than when the ad does all the work.

What Do I Need To Know?

When marketing a product or concept that is either complex or complicated to use, begin by asking yourself some questions.

If I were the customer:

- How much would I want or need to know about the product's complexity, to enable me to know if buying it would *meet my needs*?

- Which would be more important to me, what its use will do for my business or how complicated it is to use?

The key in the first question is *my* needs, not someone else's but *my* needs. If I need a lot of information, please give me that education the way a good salesperson does, a piece at a time. Resist the urge to tell it all to me in one wordy ad, because I won't read it. Keep it simple.

Educate me about one part of the technical complexity and tell me the results that it will produce for me. In the next ad in a series, repeat what you told me in the first ad, but use fewer words because I only need to be reminded. Then give the next piece of complexity and the results it will provide me.

Do this in a series of ads and I will be happy to educate myself by reading your ads. However, each ad must give me the results and let me decide if and when they meet my needs. Use the same methodology concerning its complicated use.

Remember, an ad and its message is absorbed the same way regardless of the media used to transmit it to me. E-mail, Internet, magazine, trade journal, FAX, radio, TV, and direct mail are methods; the principles do not change with different methods. Each must educate me and create or maintain a positive perception of a difference in my mind.

"Do You Remember This Ad?"

When I first began selling I became an avid reader of advertising because it was an easy way to learn what my competitors were telling my customers and prospects. I didn't just glance at or speed-read the ads; I read them for content. I checked them for accuracy and truthfulness. I did this in the library reference section. I shopped places that sold them, and I called their headquarters information desks to ask questions. Because my voice is distinctive and easy to remember I could never call the same place twice, but my wife and secretary could.

This effort, plus asking questions of their customers, enabled me to learn which competitors inflated claims a great deal and which inflated them just a wee tad. I learned over the years that the number of footnotes, amount of fine print, and point size of the fine print correlated very well with the degree of honesty in ads and brochures. I know that the U.S. Government requires disclaimers and qualifying statements in ads and brochures. What I object to is the use of pale ink colors and print that requires a magnifying glass when reading them. It sends the message or, if you prefer, creates the perception that you are dishonest or purposely leaving something out. Print these qualifiers clearly so I can read them and this won't happen. This said, you understand why I accepted when a researcher from a marketing firm called for an appointment.

He placed ads in front of me and asked:

"Do you remember this ad?"

"What is its message or what is it selling?"

My answers surprised me. I could remember every ad that depicted a woman… but I rarely remembered its message or what it was selling. At the time I was in my prime and happily married. The researcher was older than I and I respected him enough to agree to a return visit. We met three times at four to six week intervals. I learned a lot from that and at the end of the last visit, he confirmed the validity of my observations.

• Full-page ads were a waste on me, even with a female figure in them.

• Quarter page ads were more effective, but placement on the page had a great effect. The upper right quarter was most easy for me to remember. If the copy had a bearing on my business or family needs, I remembered the message and what it was selling even five weeks after I received the publication. If it didn't, I had trouble remembering it in the third week. The bottom right quarter position came in second.

- Smaller ads were more effective if placed on the right side of the page. It became apparent that I look at advertisement pages by scanning down the right side in speed reading fashion, then return to really read those that apply to my business or family needs.

- I invariably read the back page of every section in a paper and the back cover of a publication.

- If the ad contained too much copy, and/or pictures with little white space, I did not read it unless it specifically applied to my needs. It might have been very educational but I did not want to spend the time to get a full education in one sitting. I also tended not to remember it that well. However, if I thought it could be important to me, I would tear out the page and read it later; sometimes several weeks later if a deadline was not obvious. Hence, a single page or sheet describing a seminar would be read at once and either acted upon or put in the waste basket. A thick booklet describing a seminar in detail, would be carried home, read on the weekend, and given careful thought before taking action.

- I remembered small ads that appeared regularly in the same location of a periodical and knew what they were selling, if there was any chance that I might someday be interested in the product or service. In this case the presence of a female figure was usually a detriment, or at best unimportant.

- If I sensed dishonesty in the ad I remembered it easily and always negatively.

The researcher indicated that I was not unusual.

✧✧✧

Can This Be Applied To TV and Radio? Yes, Yes, Yes

The most effective radio advertisements I've ever heard were 60-second spots, which I heard while laying awake in bed after the radio alarm woke me, while I was shaving, or as I commuted to work. Radio in the office during the workday was easily tuned out by my mind.

There is no question that when I listened to these spots two or at most, three times, they became unforgettable. They contained no music or anything else to distract me from their message. They completely educated me about the product or service they were selling and where the seller was located. They were delivered at a slow pace compared with the typical radio or TV ad. There was time enough in one minute to speak understandably and let my mind picture the use of the product or enjoyment of the service. In every case, they resulted in at least one sale to me or visit to the seller by me.

These ads were effective because they were repeated on a regular schedule, at the same time of day, using the same pleasant sincere voice, at a pace that left "white space" for my mind to work on what was said. They did not have to be on the air every day, because they were easy to remember and my mind had the time to store them with "access keys." This made them cost effective. One, for a restaurant, ran from the time the place opened for business. The voice changed when the announcer died after nearly 30 years delivering the message. It is a rare restaurant that remains in business and profitable for that many years. The ad must have been cost effective.

The effectiveness resulted from allowing my mind and imagination to work. The ad creator selected the voice very carefully in all cases. There was no effort to use special effects or sounds for the sake of being "arty" with the technology. That would have distracted my mind from the important work of painting mental pictures. Consider this as you read the next true story.

"Honey, Did You See That Table?"

"What table? Where?"

"In that furniture ad that was on the screen just now. You were looking right at the TV, how could you miss it?"

"I glanced down at what the dog was doing. Why was the ad important? We aren't in the market for furniture."

"It showed a dining table with expansion leaves that are stored inside of it. The table must be round but I'm not sure of that. We've got to watch for that ad again so we see that table. It is unique."

"Which furniture store is selling the table?"

"I don't know."

We watched for the ad every evening when we watched the news. On two occasions Amy saw the ad but afterward could not remember who was selling the table. She could only tell me that the table was either round, hexagonal or octagonal, and the leaves came out of the center of the table. On the third occasion I was present...

"Look, quick... did you see the table?"

"Yes, it is interesting. The leaves must be in a pedestal, like the barrel under our kitchen table. We ought to go to the store just to see how it works."

"I agree, but I still don't know which store is selling it."

"Do you realize that you have now seen that ad four times and I've seen it once and we don't know which furniture store the ad is selling. What do you remember about the ad?"

"I'm going to use the "P" word and say I have the perception that the store sells expensive, high-end furniture.* The ad has four different furniture arrangements on the screen at once and they appear to be high quality. The table caught my attention because when it is shown it is in the center of the other four arrangements and it is the only one that moves, the leaves are rising out of the center, then it is gone. I cannot remember what the voice was saying and I was still thinking about the table when the name of the store must have come on the screen. That's the fastest 30-second ad I've ever seen."

"I've got the same mental picture you describe."

"Wes, you should talk about that ad in your book."

✧✧✧

Which of the points that the researcher proved to me is illustrated in this true story?

---

*I have used "perception" so often in our house that Amy has tried to ban its use in her hearing.

How could the ad have been made more effective?

This ad is the result of using TV for the sake of TV while attempting to save money with a short 30-second spot. The ad didn't have enough "white space" to allow us to see what it was showing. We both think, but are not certain, that there were at least two frames with four pictures each on screen before the one that showed the table and at least two frames after the table was shown; each with a different picture in each quarter. There had to have been an introductory frame and an ending frame with the store name, address, etc. Assuming these numbers are correct, each frame was on screen for about 4 seconds. This is time enough for the mind to register the picture and a message if there is only one on screen but not with four.

Consider this:

You are on a freeway driving at 60 miles an hour. You are maintaining a five-second distance between you and the car ahead of you. If you are concentrating on driving and not thinking about something else, you have a chance of reacting and stopping in time when the car ahead suddenly stops. If you're not concentrating you will, at best, have a severe jolt and not be able to remember exactly what happened. How often are you and I concentrating on the TV screen enough to sort out and remember four different scenes during an ad?

The ad missed its most important point…the table that moved and grew larger, seemingly with effortless grace. That table scene shown full screen without voice over, followed by a store name and address frame with voice over, would have pulled people into the store. That is the purpose of an ad. Get me into the store and there is a 55 to 60 percent chance I will buy something on impulse.*

---

*Remember the "wild card" in the buying process.

What Does The Ad *Really* Say?

I will always remember one TV ad that featured a large animal and a message delivered in a very pushy manner. This store's ad, with the animal, was repeated constantly with different products. It quickly educated me on one key point:

If you come here we will succeed in convincing you to buy whether you want to or not.

I never went to this place because I don't like to struggle when buying or selling. One of our sons visited the store when he needed a product it sold and returned totally distrustful of the selling team and its approach. He went elsewhere to buy. This does not mean the ad is poorly done. It simply shows that you as a marketing person must know what perceptions it creates and if they fit the market you are targeting.

The ad was very effective for two generations of company owners. This illustrates the fact that different ad messages appeal to different people. Those who find this store a fun place in which to buy would be bored to tears with the establishments I like.

As a marketing person, you must be sensitive to the personality and character of the people in the business you are promoting. The marketing message, the people in the business, and their way of conducting business must match. If they do not, failure will result because the perception of a difference created by the ad does not match up with the perception of a difference created by the people in the business. The ad attracts a specific buyer profile. If buyers in that profile do not find the same difference when they come to the business, they will leave without buying. The people in the business, not the product, make the difference.

Remember *The New Motorcycle* story in Chapter 2? I visited those two stores several more times. In one store the people create two perceptions. The first perception is that they are sincerely glad you came to see them. The second perception is that they are a class act and can be trusted to provide flawless service at prices that are profitable to you and them. They maintain and strengthen these perceptions consistently, every time you visit the store.

In the other store the people also consistently create two perceptions in my mind. One, that I am a chicken ready to be plucked of its feathers; and two, that they will deliver as good service as I make them deliver. I represent a different buyer profile from that of their typical customers. The two stores sell the same brand of motorcycle.

The store I think of as the chicken plucker sells more cycles, but services fewer cycles than the other store. Its pricing on new and used cycles is perceived as flexible. Some people who purchased their cycle at the chicken plucker, did so to get a better deal on the purchase. They then drive to the store with the POD of a class act and trustworthiness for maintenance and repair. This store sells fewer cycles and does not cut deals. It tends to be perceived as higher priced for both purchases and service.

Both stores are very successful, profitable businesses. The people make the difference. The customers they acquire are from different buyer profiles. The advertising and marketing effort must be different for the two stores.

✧✧✧

Honest Advertising Pays. It's Your Responsibility

Honesty in advertising requires that the message educates me, the buyer, about the philosophy and character of the people in the store, as well as about the product they sell. I don't like surprises. Most people don't. A gunslinger enjoys the challenge in a store where he knows in advance that he should stay close to a door with his back to the wall. Honest advertising will bring people who like this challenge to the store that offers it, and will drive those who like less of a challenge to another store.

Honest marketing people will educate the owners of each type of store about their differences and the different buyer profiles they attract. Because of this they are not competitors even if they are located in the same block on the same side of the street. Both will prosper if the advertising is honest. When either one attempts to sell to both buyer profiles, it will fail because you cannot straddle a barbed wire fence for long, without pain!

Honest advertising creates trust, the trust that works so well for the second motorcycle store and its service department. Dishonest advertising destroys trust and changes a positive perception of a difference into a negative one. When you write your next marketing brochure remember that we all remember and talk about a good business experience for 18 months and a bad one for 21 years.* You need not take my word for this, just listen to the person who complains about a product or company. It will not matter if the incident occurred last week or 12 years ago. In every case it will turn out that the person has the perception they were lied to or were "talked into" believing a lie. Every time that person tells the story it makes another potential buyer of your company's products distrustful of your company.

---

*A research study involving over 2,400 people, done in the 1980s revealed this. Modern medical and psychological research shows the brain builds stronger pathways to unpleasant or painful memories than to happy ones.

If your company is small, this continued negative storytelling has the power to bring it to its knees. If your company is a large corporation, chances are no one in management will care. I remember a corporation with over 26 million customers that "woke up" when someone in its organization noticed that it had lost one million customers. They had left, one by one in 12 months, and they were continuing to leave at the same rate without new customers replacing them. Size does not protect you when your POD turns negative. Dishonesty is very effective at creating a negative perception of a difference.

Choosing An Advertising Or Marketing Agency

It is my hope that at this point you have come to accept the premise that selling is a face-to-face educational process and that marketing is selling without face-to-face contact. It took me over half a lifetime in selling and marketing to grasp this. When I did, it quickly became obvious that a lot of marketing efforts missed the mark and were ineffective because the marketing people creating them had never been high producers in face-to-face selling. I learned that having carried the title of sales representative doesn't necessarily make a person a great marketing person. This story in which I am the listener, not a speaker, is a good illustration of this.

> *"One of the most ineffective marketing groups I've seen was in a corporation that staffed the marketing department with sales managers and managers of branch sales offices."*

> *"I'm surprised at that. I would expect people with field sales experience to be effective in marketing. Did you ever figure out why it didn't work?"*

"Yes. It took some time, discrete questioning, and a search of personnel files to discover that all of the ineffective marketing people had been "promoted" to the marketing department after essentially failing in the field. Their performance as sales representatives had been average at best. They were promoted to sales or branch management because of their years of service. When the person who promoted them realized it was a mistake, he'd sell the marketing department the idea of hiring them and then tell the individual it was a promotion. This was the old practice of trying to find a place where the person would fit. Trouble was, these people were low on imagination and high on not rocking the boat.

The two people who were effective in Marketing had been high performers in sales and sales management and had asked for positions in marketing. They knew what the top performing salesperson needed to help educate the prospect and they knew what the prospect would read and find useful in the buying process. Best of all, they knew how to sell their ideas to top management."

"What was the result?"

"The two individuals carried the Marketing Department. They came up with the ideas; everybody else used them as their own and implemented them. It worked until the two of them got tired and resigned. Then it quickly became apparent that the wrong people were left."

If you have hiring responsibility for Marketing, carefully check the qualifications of those presented to you as good additions to your staff. Selling and Marketing are both educational processes. In my experience, mediocre salespeople are either poor educators or lazy.

Marketing needs good educators. They don't have to be former salespeople.

The client company had developed an application software package and was selling it quite successfully. The CEO hired us to find and smooth out rough spots that he was not aware of. His marketing staff consisted of two people who produced attractive, effective brochures, advertisements for trade journals, and creative sales aids. These two people also made selling presentations to prospects and answered their questions with enthusiasm. They knew how the software package worked, how it would be used by the prospect, and the results from its use. They were great educators.

They had no selling, as in professional sales, experience, but both had been teachers, one in the elementary grades, one teaching English composition and writing skills in high school. They left teaching because they could earn more in industry. They'd found their way to this company by "accident."

I always remember these two stories when a client asks me to help them find people to staff the marketing department or help them select an advertising agency. I believe the secret to success in either case is in these two stories. They support the premise that Buying, Marketing, and Selling are *educational* processes. Good salespeople and good marketing people are teachers, educators, and listeners. They are also loaded with enthusiasm. This is what you want in an advertising agency.

After, and not before, you have read the proposal submitted by an advertising agency, ask the leader five questions:

1. Who on the team handling our account has a marketing degree?

2. Who on the team has been a teacher in elementary or high school?

3. Who on the team has done face-to-face selling?

4. What product did they sell and were they average or above average producers?

5. Would you hire them to sell your product? Why?

When you ask these questions be poker faced and very observant of how they are answered, as in tone of voice, shifting of eyes, and the length of time for thought before the answer is given.

The sequence of these questions is important. The first is easy to answer and puts the leader at ease, the answer may be in the boiler plate of the proposal so if you've read it, precede the questions with a disclaimer such as, "I'm not sure I saw the answers to a couple of questions I want answered so please bear with me," then ask the questions. The second, third, and fourth questions may not be answered in the proposal but they will not be threatening. When you ask the fifth question do you hear a rehearsed answer, quickly given, or a thoughtful, sincere response you can trust?

If your "liver quivers," or you experience a moment of doubt, break off the interview and ask another agency for a proposal. You are going to spend a ton of money and experience success or failure as a result of this decision, so make sure you are comfortable with the leader and the team.

If you are not comfortable with an individual on the team, ask the leader to make a change. You will be most successful if you remember you are hiring these individuals to teach and educate for you.

Consider these thoughts. A marketing degree is no assurance of effectiveness in marketing or ad creation, particularly if it is not accompanied with selling experience in your product or industry. The two together can be an excellent combination. Based on the stories above, successful selling or teaching experience will be more useful than a degree in marketing and/or sales. Teaching in a college or university will be less desirable unless your product is targeted at people with post-graduate degrees. Even then, the person who can communicate easily with high school seniors will write more easily absorbed material than one that does not.

Can Anyone Understand It?

Will people, other than you and those who created the radio or TV spot, understand the words?

Will they know what that beautiful scenery shot is saying about your product?

Does your ad make people want to drive at dangerous speeds on curving roads and kill themselves or others?

Does your ad educate them about how much fun and satisfaction they'll have driving your car safely?

Which message do you want the ad to communicate?

Show the spot to ordinary people, one at a time, and ask them what it makes them want to do.

It's Your Responsibility

In Marketing you define the product. You do this with research, with questions, and listening to the customer. The customer is the Distributor, the Dealer, and the ultimate user of the product.

In Marketing you are responsible for the message customers hear. This means you must educate, train, and support the people in Sales and Customer Care. You must listen to what they are telling the customer and to them when they tell you what the customer is saying. You must use this input to help Engineering, Design, and Production keep the product in step with customer needs and wants. It's your responsibility to listen, *hear*, and then teach.

The motorcycle company is more than 100 years old because its message has been consistent and honest. Consistent and honest enough to earn and keep the trust of engineers, designers, production people, salespeople, dealers, and the customers who ride those cycles all over the world. In your company, in Marketing, it's your responsibility!

CHAPTER 6

Selling

The Basics Of The Profession

Selling is the third key block in the business arch. It is a required part of the buying process whenever interaction with a human is necessary for satisfactory completion of the buyer's education.

When practiced ethically, selling is an honorable profession and noble calling that makes a positive difference in the lives of many people. It is richly rewarding and deeply satisfying. It is both a process and an art, in which success depends more on basic principles than skillful use of techniques.

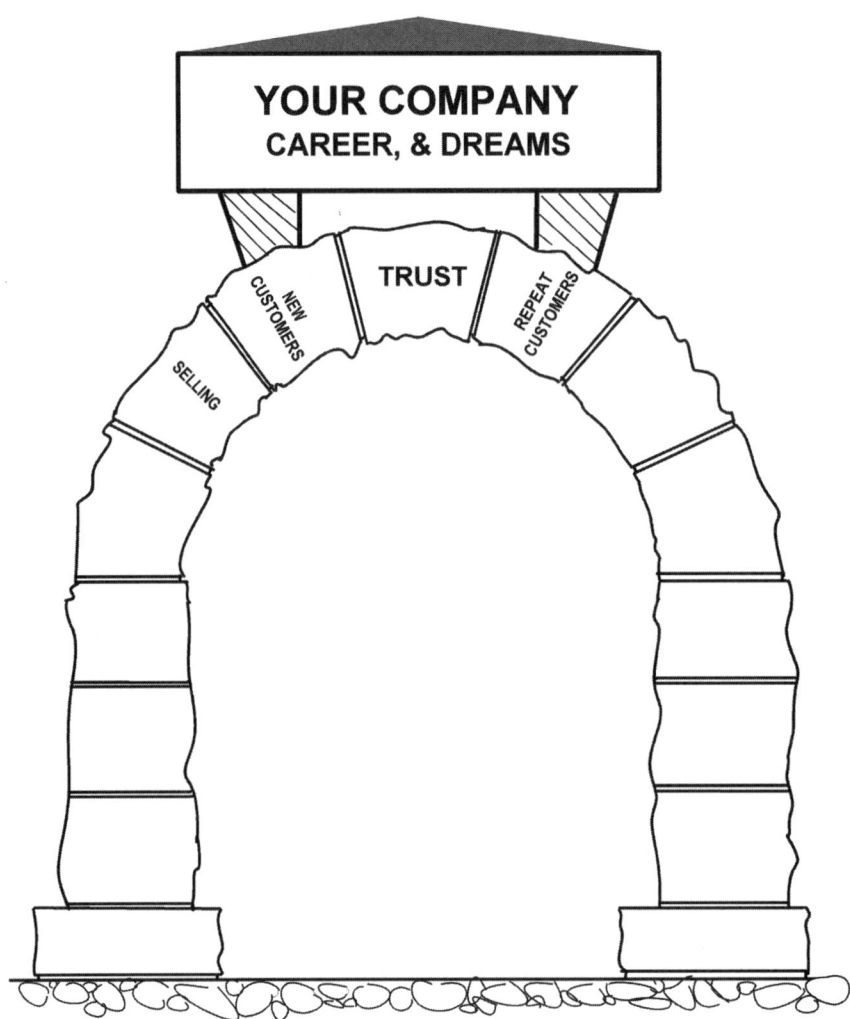

The Business Arch

Thoughts To Ponder

You live in modern times. You picked this book up in the library, or bookstore, or downloaded it because you hoped to learn something that will help you in your work. You have probably enjoyed the chapters on buying and marketing. Now you are wondering how it all applies in today's modern world. I understand how you feel.

When I went to my only formal sales class, Dan Merrick was teaching us how to sell in a modern world.* The stories in this book actually happened over a period of 65 years, yet what they teach is totally valid as you read this in a much more modern world. Why? To answer, it is important to examine what has and has not changed.

What Has Changed?

When Dad started selling in Minnesota, electricity was only available in cities and towns. There was no electricity in the countryside. Making telephone calls involved cranking the handle on the phone to get the attention of a live operator, telling her the number you wanted to call to and waiting for her to manually set up a connection. When you cranked the phone to get her attention you also got the attention of any of the six or seven other phones sharing the "party line" with you. When your phone rang you listened for the specific sequence of long and short rings that meant the call was for you. You also knew who else on your "party line" was getting a call. You were free to pick up the earpiece and listen in. A private line was astronomical in cost. Only the wealthy had private lines.

*Please see Acknowledgements at the end of this volume.

Telemarketing didn't exist, but a first class letter mailed almost anywhere in Minnesota before noon would reach an address in Minneapolis the next day. This was possible because every passenger train had a mail car in which postal employees worked sorting the mail as the train roared along at 50 to 80 miles an hour. These mailmen picked up outgoing mail, on the fly, as they passed through communities and dropped mail sacks filled with mail for the community.

In selling, up to 75 percent of all sales situations began with a cold, unannounced, no appointment, face-to-face call. The others were typically set up with a letter followed by a phone call. Long distance calls were so expensive it was often more economical to drive to a town and cold call on businesses.

When I began my professional sales career, cold calling on businesses was still the easiest way to open up a territory. I progressed from cold calling to using letters to set up appointments with prospects, and used standing appointments for calls on established customers. My experience with personalized letters was not exciting at first. When I learned to write them so they created a positive perception of a difference, they made it possible to talk with a person on a follow-up phone call and set up an appointment.

At first, the appointment was always for a face-to-face call. I changed that when I fully understood the perception of a difference and the selling process. I then asked for an appointment to talk on the phone for 45 minutes, the time I would use in a face-to-face call. E-mail then replaced the phone and letter mail for setting up appointments. At the time I write this, letter mail is slow and unpredictable and telephone/wireless has been so overworked that telemarketing is declining in effectiveness. As communication speeds advance and costs decline, video sales calls will come into common use. Indeed, that may be the case as you read this.

With all these changes in methods and communication tools, why are these stories still valid? Because of what hasn't changed.

What Hasn't Changed

I am writing this because people like you and me haven't changed. We still fall in love, dream dreams, hope, strive to make dreams come true, form perceptions, and make decisions the same way our great, great, great, great-grandparents did. We are, by and large, better educated and may be more intelligent. We often use more sophisticated tools, but our emotions, wants, and needs have not changed.

Perhaps by the year 2100 we will be able to instantly learn everything needed for a buying decision, but until then the messages in these stories are valid. Though they are all written in the first person, the "I" is many different people and most names are fictitious, chosen at random. Exceptions to this rule are those who repeatedly played a powerful role in my life who I have listed in the Acknowledgments section. In those stories I experienced personally, I use Wes, my nickname, and Amy my wife's nickname. What you read in these stories is the experience and wisdom of many people like yourself. They tell you much more than how to sell a product. Apply them to your own life situation and technology in your quest for happiness and success.

Principles vs. Techniques

"Now as to you going into sales, I never worked harder than when I was selling; I never had more fun than when I was selling; and remember, they have never repealed the Law of Averages. Love, Dad."

This is how Dad ended a long letter in response to a letter from me in which I told him I was leaving industrial management to enter professional sales. He did not mention selling until the very end of that letter, a fact that has always interested me.

Dad's selling approach included:

- Honesty

- Knowledge about the products he sold:

  - Their strengths and weaknesses in various applications.

  - About competing product's strengths and weaknesses in various applications,

  - About salespeople he competed with, their own and their employer's policies,

  - About his customers, their businesses, markets, and industries.

- Timely communication with customers, suppliers, employees.

- Always selling what was best for the customer, not himself.

- Fair pricing that yielded a fair profit and paid for real customer support after the sale.

- Consistency in all of the above.

These are the basic *principles* of selling success. They are not techniques.

Dad's formal education ended with eighth grade in a one-room schoolhouse in central Minnesota. He never attended a course on selling, or starting and running a business. I cannot remember seeing any books on these subjects in his office or our home. Yet he became nationally recognized for his approach to selling and his success in business. He did it all without leaving the area of his birth or the little town which nurtured him and his family. He sold with the same success in major metropolitan areas as in that town that has now grown to a population of 2,345 people.

I was with Dad until I went into the Army Air Corps at age 18. Much later in life, I realized that he had taught me all the *principles* of selling without my being aware of it. He taught me the principles in his sayings, which stayed in my mind and guided me ever after.* The principles are not the same as selling techniques. The principles explain why the techniques work. When you know the why, you are able to choose the techniques that best fit a given selling situation. Principles are universal, as in the last sentence in Dad's letter; "they have never repealed the Law of Averages." They apply to both selling and marketing.

Professional Selling Requires Assets

I have had the wonderful privilege of working with several hundred professional salespeople and have played the role of prospect and buyer in the many routine acquisition activities included in daily life. That experience has led me to conclude that successful and happy salespeople have six assets.

---

*His sayings are used where appropriate and are listed in the back.

1. They like and enjoy people. This enables them to hear as well as listen, with empathy.

2. They understand the perception of a difference and want to make a difference.

3. They enjoy and accept responsibility, wear it easily, and take the risks it requires.

4. They have enthusiasm, energy, and optimism.

5. They have perseverance and the personal organization to make it effective.

6. They are learners.

I have not included honesty and ethics in this list because you can be dishonest and unethical *and* successful in sales as long as you have the breath and energy to keep running….

Remember, your unhappy customers will never run out of breath chasing you and a bad reputation will never fade away.

Selling Is A Profession

If your work consists of helping people, on a personal basis, to make a buying decision, you are in the profession of selling. It does not matter if you produce and deliver the product yourself or only send the order to someone who has that responsibility. It does not matter if you do your selling using the telephone, instantaneous two-way Internet conversation, in a retail store, as a server in a restaurant, or in a corporate boardroom. Selling is an honorable profession, as honorable as you make it.

Four Levels

There are four levels within the profession of sales with corresponding levels of income for the salesperson. You can enter the profession at the first level with no training and no experience, as I did, and grow to the fourth: the highest earning level. The second level, where most people enter the profession, requires education, training, and skill that you develop with practice, over time. The third and fourth levels require the insight and judgment that can only be acquired with experience.

Sales Levels

The Order Taker	Talks to the lowest level of buying power, conversation includes the weather, number of units ordered last month, how many do you need now, etc.
The Peddler	Talks to line management and the purchasing agent about product and price.
The Consultant	Talks to staff management. They are concerned about profit and/or expense reduction. The consultant talks about solutions that will increase profit or reduce expense.
The Counselor	Talks to senior executives who are interested in bottom line results. The counselor salesperson works to develop a proposal to affect the bottom line, listens a lot, and asks questions to help the person see the complete picture. The relationship with the executive can become quite far-reaching.

Complex vs. Simple Sales Situations Defined

The simplest sales situation is one in which the buyer makes a purchase with no contact or input from others and has sole responsibility for the outcome. The salesperson has only the buyer to educate and the buyer makes the decision to buy without any influencer, other than the salesperson. In my experience this situation never occurs.

Realistically, there is more than one person involved on the buyer's side in every sales situation. The complexity of a sales situation is directly related to the number of people whose lives will be impacted by the decision to buy. Those who will be heavily impacted will have both yes and no power in the sale whether they are visible to the salesperson or not. Some will not be able to say yes but will be able to say no, and some can only influence the decision. The greater the number of people affected, the longer the decision time will be. The absolute size of the sale price has little impact on the complexity of the sale, so long as it is within the "pen power" of the actual buyer.*

---

*The person that appears to be the buyer may not have the authority to spend the amount required. In a corporation with annual sales of one billion dollars, the Treasurer had authority ("pen power") to spend up to $500,000 on any one purchase, the President could approve up to $750,000 and the CEO's limit was one million dollars. The finance committee of the Board of Directors approved any single purchase above one million dollars.

Two Divisions

There are two divisions in the profession:

1. Tangible, the selling of products, e.g., vehicles, services.

2. Intangible, the selling of ideas, e.g., insurance, advertising, services.*

The principles are the same in both as are the techniques; however, they require somewhat different skills. You must decide which you prefer and are happiest with. The distinction is not always clean cut, as you will see later, but it is important to your selling success. You will learn which is best for you from experience and personal introspection.

Pursuers And Gardeners

In each of these divisions there are two types of selling situations. When I began selling they were referred to as "inside" and "outside," but that does not fully describe the difference for me. The inside salesperson was one who waited for prospects to come in the door, and the outside salesperson went to the prospect's location to initiate the sales discussion. In my experience, selling and leading teams of salespeople, the correct way to decide which is your forte is to determine if are you a pursuer/hunter, or a gardener/farmer. A gardener is not happy making cold calls on the phone or via written communication.

---

*Services are in both divisions because the real product of a service is an intangible idea. The story about selling plants in a later chapter illustrates this.

Pursuers are comfortable doing this: to them it is a challenge that the gardener thinks of as a difficult chore. The choice is not either-or, because you can be some of both. The important thing is to know who you are and choose accordingly. Selling should be fun for you, as it was for Dad and every successful salesperson I've worked with.

It Makes No Difference

Everything you and I will discuss in the balance of this book applies equally to both types of selling situations and all products and services that you may sell in your lifetime. The principles are essential to success in all cases. Some techniques are more successful with some products than others and individual people are more comfortable with some techniques than others. Your experience will be the deciding factor.

We will consider pursuers and their experiences first. It is easier to learn from them because their sales tend to be complex rather than simple, involving multiple contacts with the buyer. Long sales cycles give the salesperson a chance to recover from some mistakes. The inside salesperson is more often involved in a higher percentage of zero tolerance, "do it right the first time," short duration, less complex sales situations.

Selling Is A Process

Selling is an educational process in which the salesperson and buyer take turns being student and teacher. The most consistently successful salespeople I've known and observed in action were methodical and enthusiastic in both roles. Many salespeople don't think of themselves as teachers; I'm certain my Dad didn't, but you will be more successful, as I was, when you understand this.

You are the student when you ask questions to learn the buyer's needs and listen to the answers. You are the teacher when you explain how your product, idea, or service will satisfy those needs. It is an iterative process, which continues until both you and the buyer fully understand how your product will work in the buyer's situation. When the benefits are sufficient, a mutually satisfying sale automatically results. Believe it or not, it happens without the use of special techniques or "closing" routines. The second wonderful result of this process is that usually you and the buyer know early in the process if your product cannot satisfy the buyer's needs. As a result you and the buyer part company as friends, and you quickly move on to a new opportunity.

Now let's see how this all worked in the lives of many successful salespeople.

Chapter 7

People Educating Each Other

Selling is an educational process that the professional salesperson executes effortlessly every day.

Learning how to do it well is a lifetime effort. It has created a market for countless books,

recordings, and seminars. In addition, many companies develop extensive training programs to

ensure the success of their salespeople. All of these are valuable.

My experience in a company sales school was invaluable but the education I was given by sales

veterans I worked with was what really made me successful. It was informal, it happened every

week, and I soaked it up. As you will see in this and the next chapter, it was all about educating and

using the power of the perception of a difference. The stories tell it all.

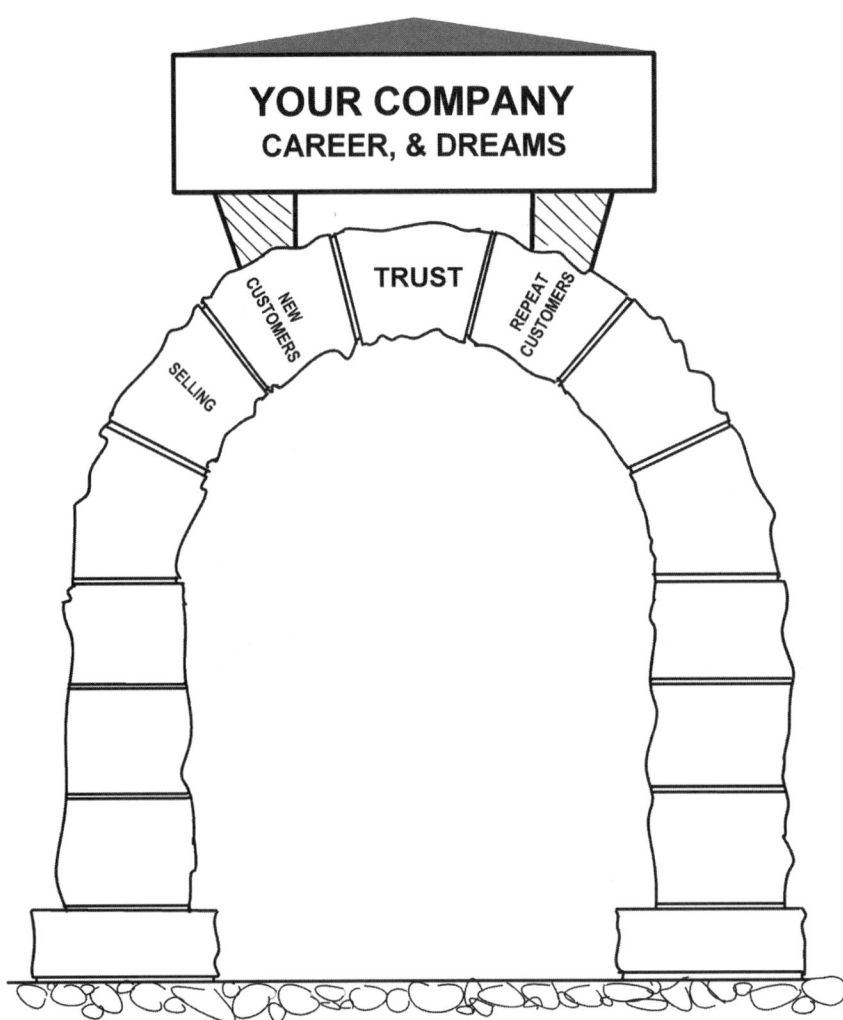

The Business Arch

The Making Of A Professional

I experienced only two selling courses in my life. The first was the single day I spent with the brush company district manager, the second was four weeks in the business systems company sales course.

The brush company had built its success on consistently high quality products and polite sales representatives. Those were the days when TV sets were rarely seen, vacuum cleaners were expensive and inefficient, and the majority of homes had "only one income" issues.

Door-to-door salesmen were almost as common then as telephone marketers would be later. Every sales call was a "cold call." Individual sales styles ranged from polite and soft-spoken to extremely aggressive and manipulative. Products sold door-to-door included herbs and spices, pots and pans, fine china, brushes, toothpaste, floor wax, flower seeds, encyclopedias, vacuum cleaners, and many other items.

The salesman had to get the homemaker's attention, convince her to listen, look, and perhaps see a demonstration and sign an order for later delivery or pay cash for immediate delivery. In my experience, in fully 40 percent of these sales calls, all the above steps were completed on the front entry of the home with the screen door closed between the homemaker and salesman. Saleswomen were almost unheard of and "sales" was not considered a desirable occupation for your sons. Hence, the brush company district manager spent the day teaching me how to do everything that would cause the homemaker to open the screen door and invite me in. I didn't realize, at that time, that he was teaching me how to create a positive perception of a difference in the first 30-seconds after I knocked on the door.

I must have learned well because I was very successful at it. However, I came to dislike selling very much because often I would watch the homemaker scrounge for the "mad money" or shake out the contents of a piggy bank when I delivered the order. This made me feel guilty. When the load of guilt became too heavy, I quit.

Look At The Person On Each Side Of You

I went to the business systems company sales course with real trepidation. I had joined because my perception of Ralph Sweeney, the District Manager, was that he was a person I could trust so much that somehow selling would be OK for me after all, just because he said so.

The first hour in sales class was unforgettable. Dan Merrick had been a successful salesperson for this company. He was also a gifted, enthusiastic teacher. He combined what I had learned about polite, friendly selling with a measured, carefully timed, use of aggression. He believed that selling was a high order profession and that only the best could become sales professionals. Perhaps 20 minutes into that first day, he said,

> *"Look at the person on each side of you. Two years from now only one of the three of you will be in sales."*

It was a personal challenge for me. I intended to be the one out of three.

It was different than selling brushes, which are a tangible. We were selling systems that we would design to solve the customer's problems. We would be paid commission on the tools and supplies used by the system. Our real product was intangible: our ideas. The more complex the

The Perception of a Difference

system, the more this was true. The simple systems were primarily tool sales. To succeed you had to know how the tools could be applied to a customer's business.

Education And Perception Creation

It was essential that you be able to demonstrate the tool, as the customer's employee would use it, while relating it to the prospect's business functions. Above all the demo had to make it look easy and simple so both the person who would sign the order and those who would use the tools could imagine themselves doing it easily. Whenever possible they were asked to repeat the demo themselves while you explained what the system did for them and the business. The practice with the tool was training; when coupled with your explanation it became education in the purest sense, but Dan never referred to it in that way. The demo was also a perception-creation process. The decision to buy hinged on that perception coupled with a full understanding of how and why it would save time, or money, or frustration, or improve sales, or production, or all of the above.

Repetition And Practice

Dan told us everything he was going to tell us about the products and tools in the first week. The following three weeks he repeatedly applied the product information to actual applications and told us a few hundred other things about selling. He repeated, in his own words, all the selling principles contained in Dad's sayings; and he taught us every selling technique you've ever heard or read. He made it clear that if you got the prospect to fully teach you about his/her business needs and designed a system that would truly help, you would *not* need the techniques.

The demonstration was the way to show that the system would truly help the customer. Therefore, he made us practice sales calls and demonstrations for two hours after dinner every evening, four evenings a week. I got so uptight doing it that I got sick to my stomach if I ate before the practice sessions so I would snack afterward. I've always wondered about this because I had never had much stage fright before taking this class; and when I went into the territory, demos were fun for me.

Every Thursday we dressed up for cocktails and dinner with the wives of the company's executives. Dan served as bartender at these occasions. On Friday we were back in class and spent the weekend practicing demos and studying system design. That four-week sales class was both an exhilarating and grueling experience. As I drove home I wondered out loud if I would like selling. Six months later as I sat reading the company newsletter, Amy said,

"You'll never quit selling."

"Why do you say that?"

"You enjoy it too much to quit."

I remembered Dad's letter: "I never had more fun than when I was selling."

Neither have I.

Dan's prediction was correct. Two years later only five of my classmates were still in sales.

The first day in the office after class, Ralph informed me that I would be a successful salesperson. This was in the report he had received from Dan. It turned out that the executive wives had written their personal impressions of us after each Thursday evening dinner and produced a report for our managers. They said I was courteous, respectful, at ease, and visited with each of them each week. They reported that I had "class" and would be accepted at high organizational levels. Dan's report included my preference in cocktails and wine, that I was discrete in my use of alcohol* and thorough in my class work. Ralph then said:

"I have no doubt that you will succeed as a salesperson, but you should remember that if you become a top producer you should not expect to be promoted to sales or branch manager. Ninety-five percent of all top salespeople fail in sales management. I am not certain why this is true, but I know from experience that it is. For now, just do your best and enjoy yourself."

He then asked me to work in our booth in a major business systems conference opening the next day. During my first shift, two men came to my station and looked at the display and my demo, which I did flawlessly. One asked;

"Why should I buy this?"

Without conscious thought I gave him the four key benefits from its use. He took out his business card.

"Call me on Tuesday for an appointment."

---

*Without our knowing, Dan recorded what we drank and how much as he served us.

When they were gone I thought, "Where did what I said come from?"

It came from Dan's constant repetition and the practice sessions. I decided then that I would practice every day. I still practice, speaking out loud in front of a mirror, before each presentation.

Education Tells Why; Training Tells How

Dan's methodology caused me to take ownership of what he was teaching. This gave me the ability to use it in my words, my style of selling. He had educated me, which is far different than training. He had taught the "why" about our products and selling. Training teaches the "how," the techniques. Dan combined training and education. He spent four weeks teaching us why and how to create positive perceptions. Once we knew why, we were able to strengthen them in the prospect's mind. Dan never used the word perception, but he knew the prospect would make decisions based on those perceptions.

The "how" began with what we wore, how we walked, the words and phrases we used, everything that creates the positive or negative perception in our mind during those first crucial five seconds. Dan made it clear that the first moments in view of anyone in the prospect's place of business were important. He knew that most of the class members had no experience in selling. Some had been peddlers, as when I sold flower and vegetable seeds as a kid. My experience selling brushes put me ahead of most of the class in terms of experience. Maybe that was why I was scared of selling full time and they did not seem to be.

When I sold brushes I was on straight commission. The only time I received funds was when I collected upon delivery. I paid all my expenses and paid for the brushes when I ordered them. If the customer decided not to take delivery I owned the inventory and had to sell it to someone else, but at that time I only had myself to worry about. Now I was married to Amy, we had three children and another on the way to worry about, and I was the breadwinner. This is probably why I became successful in the profession of sales. I now know that my success came as a result of doing everything Dan had told us to do. I had responsibilities.

You've Got To Organize Your Time And Territory

When I started with this company, I received a nonrefundable starvation draw against commissions I would earn. That draw had to support my family and cover all the expenses of working the territory. Regardless of how much I sold, I would get no more than that draw until I chose to go on straight commission. The decision would be irrevocable: If you don't sell, you don't eat.

Ralph gave me a territory that included a piece of the city and a lot of open space with old, slowly growing communities scattered throughout. These communities were home to many smaller businesses and a few quite large corporations. Existing customers in the territory provided repeat business as they reordered tools and supplies for their systems.

I studied the map, knowing that I had to pay for my gas and any entertaining and remembering things Dan had said in class:

> *"A face-to-face call should not last more than one hour; 45 minutes is ideal. Your customer/prospect is too busy to spend more time with you. You have to make each call worth the time they spend with you.*

"If you make eight face-to-face selling calls a week, you will make a living.

If you make 12 face-to-face selling calls a week, you will make a better living.

If you make 16 face-to-face selling calls a week, you will make a very good living.

If you make 20 face-to-face selling calls a week, you will be affluent.

"These calls must be divided between selling and customer support.

"A selling call is for the purpose of converting a prospect into a customer with a signed order, or getting an order for an entirely new application from an existing customer.

"A customer support call is for the purpose of maintaining your relationship with the customer, checking up on the way your present applications are being used, and training new people in the use of the application so its benefits remain in place. This ensures you of repeat tool and supply orders. Every customer support call ends with a discussion of the health of the customer's business with the intent of knowing when an additional application will help the customer.

"The frequency of customer support calls is governed by the current and potential value of the customer.

"A customer who gives you $50.00 a year in commissions is worth one face-to-face call and one or two phone calls a year. The phone calls tell you if an extra call to explore a new application is in order. That one face-to-face call is by appointment.

"A customer who gives you $500.00 a year in commission is worth one call a quarter because there is a real possibility new applications will develop. You must be a businessperson in deciding on the call frequency for each customer. You will have customers that warrant one call a month. It is a business decision.

"Entertaining is a business decision. A $1,000.00 commission may be worth a lunch; a much larger one that will repeat every year is worth dinner on or near the customer's birthday.

"Divide your territory into sections with the size of each determined by how far you can drive during lunch hour. You want to be able to leave a call at one edge of the section at 12:30 and arrive at another call at the other end of the section by 1:30. You eat while driving and you eat light. You do this so you can make maximum use of prime selling time."

Territory Sectioned By One Hour's Driving Time

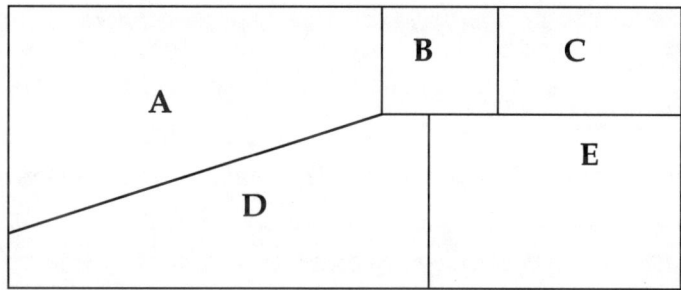

"There are 16 prime selling hours in a week."

He drew the following chart on the board.

Prime Selling Hours

Monday	Tuesday	Wednesday	Thursday	Friday
	9:30 a.m.	9:30 a.m.	9:30 a.m.	9:30 a.m.
	11:30 a.m.	11:30 a.m.	11:30 a.m.	11:30 a.m.
1:30 p.m.	1:30 p.m.	1:30 p.m.	1:30 p.m.	
3:30 p.m.	3:30 p.m.	3:30 p.m.	3:30 p.m.	

"You see that there are two hours of prime selling time in the morning, Tuesday through Friday and two hours in the afternoon Monday through Thursday. These are the hours you spend working on new business, new customers. Monday morning and Friday afternoon are spent planning, making appointments two and three weeks out, and confirming appointments for the coming week. Prospects are busy reading the mail and planning the week on Monday morning. On Friday afternoon they are trying to clear the desk so they can be home for the weekend.

"If you spend 45 minutes on a call and plan your calls so you can get to the next one in 15 minutes, you can make 16 selling calls a week. Your customer service calls are all made before nine-thirty in the morning and after three-thirty in the afternoon.

"Schedule all of one day's calls in the same section of your territory. Plan your calls on a rolling three or four-week schedule.

"When a new customer signs an order, set up a standing appointment for support calls. Explain what a support call is and say 'Let's make a standing appointment for the third Tuesday of every month at 4:30. If either of us can't make it we'll call the other in advance.' Some customers will prefer a time before or after normal business hours, which is to your advantage. You choose the day so it fits in your schedule for that section of your territory. The standing appointment saves you and the customer time, and gets you closer to 20 calls a week.

"At the end of every selling call set a time for your return that fits into your next scheduled day to be in this section of your territory. Remember, besides your brain, time is your most valuable asset."

I did all these things. I soon learned that making 20 calls a week meant that I had to do systems design for new applications at night and on weekends unless I became very efficient in planning and executing. I used the standing appointment system because it saved time for both the customer and me.

I realized, later in my career, that every market has its own set of prime selling hours. They don't necessarily correspond to the ones in Dan's chart, which were perfect for selling to businesses and corporations in that cultural era, but the *principle* is valid in every market. When you insert the correct times for your market in the chart, and use Dan's other rules, you become efficient and successful in your market. This means that you can organize your work by travel time no matter what you do.

You don't fly from Phoenix to Boston for one sales call unless you can also make service calls in Boston on the same trip. Also, stop to make sales and service calls in cities on the way to and from Boston. Set your appointments in each city to keep driving time between calls at a minimum. Your time is your most valuable asset therefore you do this even if airfare costs more to stop at cities on the way to and from Boston than it does to fly to each city round trip direct.

Standing Appointments Pay Well

If you doubt the validity of the standing service appointment concept, this next story should be of interest. It was in a totally different market, different products, and different state.

> I was branch manager with responsibility for two-thirds of a Mid-Western state. I spent time with my staff members on sales and customer service calls and did some personal selling. I had standing appointments with all of my customers. To make the best use of my time, I told each customer to call my office rather than my direct phone unless it was something that simply would not wait. I told them that I would call my office, get messages, and return their call within four hours or at the end of the day. I did this to avoid interruptions during sales calls and to stay safe while driving.

On one memorable occasion I called the office at three in the afternoon and my assistant said, "Mr. MacGyver called and said that he does not want you to call him back but wants you to bring a contract for three more Model 5102s on your next scheduled visit." It was a one hundred mile drive from my office to his. He had not mentioned any need for this equipment when we had been together the week preceding.

That year my personal quota was $750,000. Each Model 5102 was priced at $169,000. Sixty-seven percent of my quota would be in my hands without disturbing my schedule and without a protracted selling effort.

Dan was correct: Standing customer service appointments do save time.

In my experience, wireless phones do not change this picture. It is still more convenient and more professional to have customers call your office and speak to a friendly live human who communicates a caring attitude than to call you on the wireless phone in your pocket. If you are driving when it rings you cannot answer it and write yourself a note safely. If you are with a customer, you cannot answer it without being rude to the person you are with. The customer calling must either leave a message on your voice mail or wait to be interrupted when you return his call. What seems like a convenience actually breaks the rhythm of the day for you and the caller. If you can't afford to pay for a person in your office you aren't a very good salesperson or you're too disorganized.

You Have To Know The Territory

I worked my butt off. I visited every existing customer in the territory and got acquainted. I wanted every one of them to know I was there to help them. I learned about their business and started a record sheet for each one. I still do this, but now it is on an electronic notebook. I found it hard to remember names, so I wrote down distinguishing things about each person after the first meeting and read those notes before I went in for the second visit. People appreciated the fact that I remembered their names months after the first call. I still have trouble remembering names and connecting them with faces.

My predecessor in the territory had not written many call reports or customer records, even though Ralph had asked for them. The call report form was in duplicate. I quickly found that if I wrote a call report that would tell me what had transpired and what had seemed important, I could save time and be more effective on the next call with the customer. That was the beginning of a career practice that satisfied my managers and improved my earnings. I sent one copy to my managers and kept the best copy in my customer file.

Customers respected me for my ready knowledge because I read those call reports when planning and executing each return call. As I read the reports from several preceding calls I could see new opportunities to serve them open up.

In those first weeks I learned a lot about my territory and even acquired a few new customers. I found that I enjoyed cold calls on small businesses, but not larger ones. The small ones were easy and fun because their problems were all the same in principle and in many details. I was comfortable with them.

The Perception of a Difference

By accident, I discovered that I was comfortable with large companies when I knew something about them in advance of the first call. I did research on each one to learn about their products, markets, number and location of plants and branch offices, and whenever possible the names of people who could be expected to have the pen power to buy a system. I also made an effort to learn about their industry if I had no experience with it. Books in the library were the best source when I began; later, time on the Internet was more productive.

This advance research became the key to success for me. First, it enabled me to determine what areas of their business could and could not benefit from the systems I sold. With this knowledge I could target the right people. Second, I could speak with just enough knowledge and confidence that the executive felt that time with me was not wasted. In reality I was asking the same questions I always asked, but I was using the language of their industry the first time I met them.

The time spent on research reduced the number of nonproductive calls per week. I knew what to emphasize in my questions, because I had a good idea of where improved methods would benefit them, even in areas they had not thought of. In essence, I knew what I was, or should be, selling to them. It is extremely important to know what you are selling.

What Are You Selling?

My territory included a garment-making section of the city. The buildings were old with no signs to identify what business, if any, was inside. I opened a door and went up the stairs into a room filled with women running sewing machines on piecework. A man came out of an office in the opposite corner, scowled, walked around the room to me, and shouted above the noise.

"What are you selling?"

"Money!"

"Come into my office."

At the end of the call he said,

"You're different. I like you."

This resulted in an order. In reality, I *was* selling money. The system I designed increased his profits so much that it paid for itself six times in a year.

My answer to his question was one I had never thought of before: It came to mind because I unconsciously thought it would appeal to the man after watching him scowl and then walk around the room to me. I started using it in other situations because it was logical when you consider that the question, "What are you selling?" is logically completed with the words "that will help me?"

We Sell Plants... Or Do We?

If you are a CEO, a President, a Principal, or a Vice President of Sales, stop reading for a moment and write down what you think your company is selling. Are you certain this is what you are selling?

It may not be what you and your sales team think it is. If it isn't you are missing sales every day as was this company:

My client had founded and built his company to several million dollars in annual sales. My charter was to help his long-term best salesman to become successful as director and builder of an enlarged sales force. I accepted the assignment with the stipulation that the founder/owner would take the course with the soon-to-be Director of Sales. I knew that would ensure success because the owner would know what the director had been instructed to do, and he would be able to understand and work with him after I was no longer there.

During the third two-day session I asked them:

"What are you selling?"

"Plants."

"What are you really selling?"

"Plants in pots and planters, placed in lobbies and offices."

"What are you selling?"

"As we just said, live plants and the service that keeps them watered, healthy, and trimmed so they look good all the time. Live plants take pollutants and carbon dioxide from the office air and return oxygen to it, so we are selling that, too."

"Do you have competitors?"

"Yes, one that operates in all of our markets and smaller ones unique to each of our markets."

"What do they sell?"

"Plants, just like us; only we do a better job of presenting it to a prospect."

"You still haven't answered my question."

"Wes, what answer are you looking for? You asked this question at the last session two weeks ago. What are we selling?"

"The image your prospect wants to create. In reality, the perception your prospect wants to create in the minds of customers and employees. Your main competitor sells plants that look like yours and wins in sales situations by saying that he's as good as you are, for less money. In the five days we have been together you have created the perception in my mind that price is key to you winning against your large competitor. This keeps your profits low.

"Teach your sales team to study the prospect's way of doing business, discover what perception the top person and employees are creating in customer's minds, and then create a plant placement design that strengthens that perception. When you present your proposal to the top person, explain the Perception of a Difference concept and how your design and plant selection makes his/her POD stronger. You'll look professional and you won't have competition because you're *selling a perception of a difference while they are selling plants. And don't forget to raise your prices to prove it. When a possible prospect asks you, "What are you selling?" say — "A stronger POD for you." Your sales team won't have trouble getting appointments to explain that statement."*

When they did this and increased their prices, despite the loud objections of the sales team, a funny thing happened; the number of sales per salesperson increased and profits soared. However, not all of the salespeople were able to make the switch from selling plants, a tangible, to selling an intangible, the idea of the perception of a difference. Those who did had much higher earnings because the commission percentage remained the same, the selling price was higher, and the number of sales, their hit ratio, increased for each of them.

Why did the hit ratio increase for those salespeople who learned to sell an intangible?

Was it honest and ethical to raise prices?

Did the price increase affect the sales hit ratio?

Before you read this you wrote down what your company is selling.

Were you correct?

This story is a great example of the importance of knowing what you are really selling. The hit ratio increased for those who learned to sell an intangible because they were directly addressing the prospect's need. They changed the questions they asked from

"Where would you like to have decorative plants?"

to,

"What do you want to communicate to your customers and employees?"

They then explained the power of the perception of a difference and educated the prospect about how this perception forms. After the prospect understood and accepted this, the rest of the sale was the sale of ideas and results, which easily justified the increase in price.

The higher price also increased sales because it created a perception of greater worth. As my Dad often said, "A man charges what he thinks he's worth."

The ideas were worth more than the plants. They triggered a new line of thought in the prospect's mind. This enabled her/him to join with the salesperson in creating a plant selection and placement design that would create a stronger perception of a difference and increase staff morale and pride. This further strengthened the perception of a difference in customer's minds. To strengthen the perception that their ideas had high worth, the salespeople were instructed to dress in good taste and in clothing of high quality. This conveyed the fact that many others were buying the salesperson's ideas.

In this last story was I selling, consulting, counseling, or all three?

The answer is all three. I was selling ideas and insights from my experience. That is the essence of consulting. The events in the story took place more than 30 years after I left Dan's sales class. It was the first part of a consulting engagement in which I began as a consultant to these two people and later became counselor to both. My business card said Consultant. It could just as well have said Salesman, Counselor Level. My progression up the four levels of selling was rewarding and emotionally satisfying. I did not plan it, but looking back I see how it happened. You can experience it, also. The next chapter shows how it happened to me and may guide you to achieve it.

Chapter 8

Moving From Peddler To Counselor

Those of us who remained in selling two years after Dan's class were successful because we were selling ideas, our own and the customer's. He had taught us to ask questions so we could learn about the prospect's needs and wants. While answering the questions, the prospect's mind was forming new insights and ideas. Our minds were, too. The results to the customer came from combining those ideas and implementing them. The ideas were embedded in the system we designed and the procedures we wrote for its use. We were consultants. We just didn't think of ourselves as such. We had reached the third level of professional sales without conscious effort.

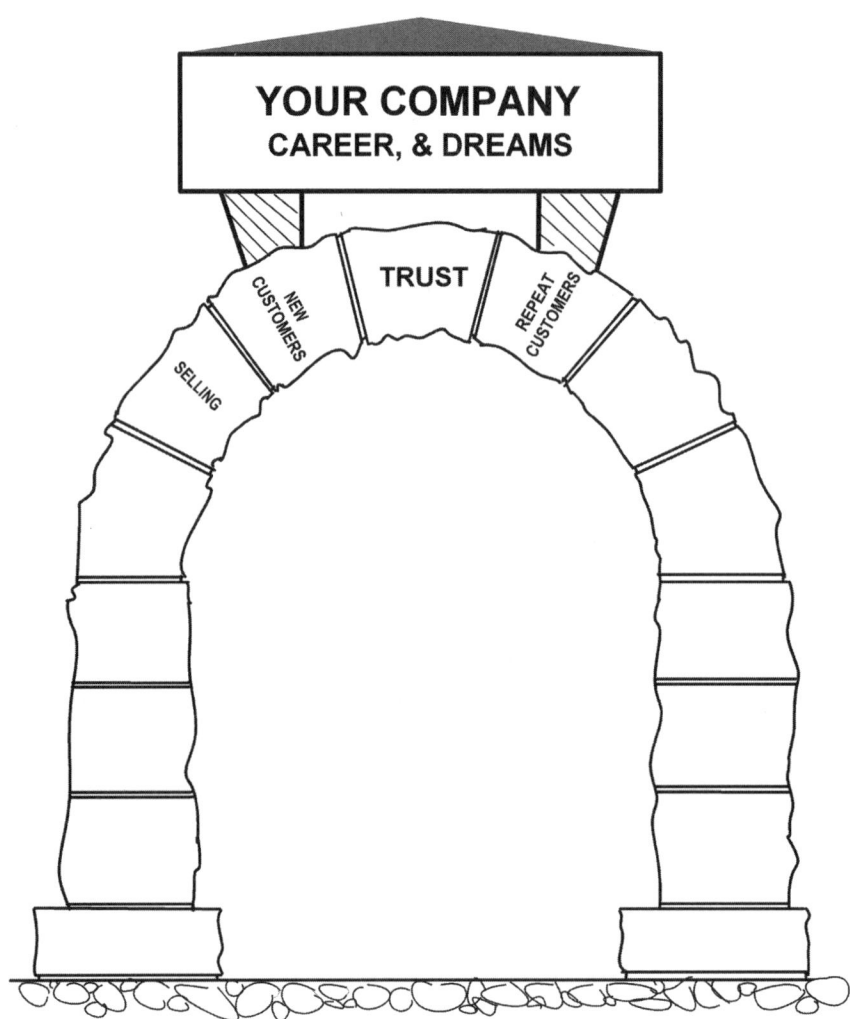

The Business Arch

Growing As A Pursuer

The salespeople in the following stories are pursuers, often called outside salespeople. I use their stories to illustrate growth through the sales levels because I knew them well, not because this growth is only available to pursuers. In Chapter 10 you will see gardeners or inside salespeople achieving the same growth. They followed the same rules for success as these pursuers.

Honesty Has Its Rewards

It was a small building in a light manufacturing area. I walked in unannounced on a cold call and was greeted by a man in his early 40s.

"How can I help you?"

"I sell custom designed systems for production control, direct cost accounting, sales analysis, and many other functions. Whom should I talk to?"

"Me, Dad, and my brother. Come in. We have time now."

"Dad" was white-haired, handsome with a firm, sincere handshake and friendly smile. The brothers were like him. They created a positive perception of a difference in my mind. I liked them instantly.

I asked questions so they could educate me about their company, markets, what had made them successful, and what their concerns were. After that I educated them on my approach to systems design. This was followed by a tour of their facility. It was small. Three identical machines pulled steel wire, flat steel, brass or aluminum from coils, and spit out hinges in any length desired into boxes ready for shipping labels.

They created tens of thousands of hinges every month in a factory with light cream floors so clean you could eat off of them. There were three employees beside themselves. It was utterly simple and profitable. They didn't need me!

Before I could tell them this, they announced an interest in a product sales analysis system. Back in the office we gathered all the information I needed to design and price a system. I gave them a date and time to be back; they agreed. We shook hands, thanked each other for time and courtesy and parted. I drove a block away, stopped, hand wrote a thank you note to be mailed later in the day, and went on to my next call.

Two weeks later I sat in the district office going through my presentation of the system I'd designed for them. I had the order written, ready for their signature. I was troubled, unhappy about the situation. Ralph Sweeney, my ever-observant District Manager, came to me.

"You don't want to make this call... Why not? Do you need more time to design the system?"

"The system is simplicity itself, just like their entire operation. It will give them everything they want and some extras I threw in."

"Then what is troubling you?"

The Perception of a Difference

"They don't need it, Ralph. They don't need it. They will be spending money they don't need to spend."

"Then tell them that. Tell them what you just said and walk out with a clear mind. It's not a big commission and you've got another proposal to present this afternoon. Do what you believe is right."

"Dad" and his sons met me at the door.

"I've come to thank you again for your courtesy and to tell you that as I looked at the finished system design and thought about all I learned during our first discussion, I cannot in good conscience sell it to you because you don't need it."

The weight was suddenly off my shoulders.

"Wes, we know that; we want it anyway. Now, please come in and show it to us, so we can get it ordered."

At noon I called Ralph to tell him what had happened.

"That's exactly what I expected."

I remembered my Dad's saying, "Don't think about your commission. Always think about what is best for the other person, and your wallet will always be full."

Was honesty involved here?

Was I both teacher and student?

Was I a consultant?

Was Customer Care evident?

I was a good student during the first call. This was proven by the fact that my system design was a perfect fit for their needs. It showed them that I was a professional, which they liked very much. My honesty in telling them my sincere concern that they didn't need the system reinforced their first perception of me. The mutual trust that resulted was wonderful. The sale resulted from mutual education and trust. No techniques were involved. I'm not sure I was a consultant. I might have been in telling them they did not need the system or was this when Customer Care was evident?

What do you think?

After my phone call to Ralph I made two additional sales calls. The first was the presentation of another new systems design. I got an order for it, also. Its commission value was five times greater than the first.

My second call was on a customer for the purpose of keeping our relationship strong. I visited him every quarter, learned about his ups and downs, and watched for new ways to help him. Once a year I would get a repeat order from him, his system was designed and installed by the salesman I had replaced in the territory. I kept his business by visiting him *when both of us knew he would not need to order.* It kept our relationship healthy and enabled him to educate me on the health and progress of his business. I would tell him about new products and what other customers were doing with them. I always left a new brochure and sent a hand-written thank you note after the call. I learned to do this from an older, very successful salesperson.

Was Customer Care involved here?

Where, when?

Customer Care was the quarterly visit scheduled when he had time to keep me current on the health of his business. Customer Care was my listening without interrupting, then asking questions to help him look at the business from a different viewpoint. Customer Care was my effort to find new ways to help him. In all of this I was showing respect and the fact that I cared about him, and his success.

He Was Blocking The Door

There are four rules for selling success in this story plus enough fun to make you remember them.

Each of us worked alone in our respective territories and only those with downtown territories visited the District Office every day, even though there was a desk, a phone, and a secretary there for us. It was a long drive for me so I did most of my system design work in my home. When I did come into the office I treasured the end of the day. Then those of us in the office, including Ralph, would go down to the street level restaurant. We would stand at the bar, enjoy one cocktail or beer and talk about our latest selling experiences and problems. Those sessions provided me a rich and invaluable education.

On one of those occasions the subject was mail order houses and their problems with order fulfillment and returns. The sheer volume of supplies these customers used to run their businesses made them valuable customers. Two of the sales veterans had designed systems for customers in this industry. They knew there were mail order houses in my territory and talked about the business and the successful systems they had installed. They educated me and got me excited about the possibilities. Their help was invaluable, and it told me I had earned their respect.

I was and am an avid gardener. We were in a new house that needed landscape plantings. Amy had been saving nursery store ads from the paper and pricing plants and shrubs. One night I searched the collection and hit pay dirt. There was a mail order source in my territory that offered a very large selection of plants and shrubs. It gave a money-back guarantee if the plants did not arrive in good condition and promised fast turnaround on orders. It also was open seven days a week for local customers. I decided to target it.

The next day I did some research on the company because the discussions at the bar indicated the system design would take a lot of time. I learned the company had been in business for over eight years, honored its guarantee, and paid its bills on time. Because my voice is very recognizable, Amy called the company to learn the name of its president.

The following week I went in and asked to see him by name. He was a confident entrepreneur, not much older than me. He knew from my business card that I sold business systems, but I started by explaining my love of gardening and our needs for the new house.

"Why ask for me when my people downstairs can answer all your questions?"

"Because I am in business like you, and like to talk with a peer. I'm interested in how you make a profit while offering low prices and guaranteed freshness, with a very perishable inventory."

"With great difficulty."

He proceeded to tell me about his business and how they had succeeded to date. In reality, they were succeeding by the brute force application of clerical staff. The seasonal nature of the business meant that new people were hired and trained twice a year. The call lasted much longer than 45 minutes. He took pleasure in sharing his problems with someone who was really interested and I took notes throughout the conversation.

"You write a lot of notes."

"I do it because I'm really interested in what you're saying and I could not possibly remember it all if I didn't. I hope you haven't minded it."

"Not at all, in fact I respect you for doing it."

"I'm going to need time to think about what you've told me. I may not be able to help you myself, but I may be able to tell you about someone else who can. In any event, I'd like to meet with you two weeks from today at nine o'clock. I'll either tell you I can't help or show you a proposed system. If it looks good to you then, will you sign an order?"

"Yes, but can we make it eleven instead of nine?"

In the car I checked my notes and made certain I could read them. This was my first big system effort. I liked the man and wanted to help him even if I, and my sales peers, could not provide an answer. Any system he implemented would be complex but it had to be simple to operate and easy to remember how to operate. The perishable nature of the product caused the complexity, the seasonal peaks and valleys made ease of operation and training essential. I knew intuitively that he would buy from me if I had the right system.

I did the work at home and put the entire system in a spiral bound presentation. It included all the forms in full size with drawings and arrows to show the workflow and what would be done at each step. Except for written verbiage it was an installation and operation manual for a system that included everything needed to order inventory, receive it, fulfill orders, and return replacements.

I took it to the office and went through the whole presentation with my sales peers and Ralph. They liked it, commented on its completeness, and cheered me on. There was excitement in the office because this was the last day of the sales year and though most of the salespeople had qualified for the 100 percent Quota Club, the office had not. If it didn't, Ralph would miss his first Club membership in 16 years. Everyone was calling customers trying to get repeat orders moved up a week or so to help him make Club. If my prospect signed an order for even a six months quantity of supplies, Ralph would make it.

No one had told me any of this for two reasons: I was six months into my first year with the company and ineligible for Club, and no one wanted me uptight when I made this presentation. I left for my 11 o'clock appointment as innocent as a lamb.

I sat beside the president and explained the flow of the system step by step. The presentation clearly showed its basic simplicity. As I turned each page I made certain he understood it completely. As we progressed, he interrupted three times to ask the cost. Each time I told him we would wait until he understood the system, then discuss cost. When I turned the last page revealing the cost for one year's supply of system components he stated:

"I like this system a lot. You have covered every trouble spot, every step in the process. I love it, but I'll start with a three-month supply. I don't want to tie up so much cash in case we can't make it work."

"I will not accept an order for three months worth because the system will not be working smoothly at the end of three months. It will be doomed to failure because in your frustration you will not order more supplies. You will have wasted the money and the team will also be frustrated and unhappy."

Well, three months is all I will buy."

I very deliberately reached down and opened my briefcase.

"Six months minimum."

I slowly put things in my briefcase.

"Three months."

"Six months minimum."

I closed the system book and picked it up.

"Three months."

I stood up and reached to shake hands.

"I thank you for your time and cooperation."

We shook hands warmly. I bent down to pick up my case from the floor and saw him moving past me headed for the door. When I stood up he was standing in front of the door with his feet wide apart and his arms stretched straight outward on either side, totally blocking the door.

"OK! Six months! I'll sign the order!"

He did. I thanked him and as we shook hands again…

"You are one tough guy."

The mental picture of him blocking the door with feet apart and arms outstretched has never faded from my memory.

I walked down the stairs, got in my car, drove silently for about a mile, pulled over, wrote a thank you note, got out of the car and hollered, "YAHOO, HOT DOG" at the top of my lungs. Then I called Amy to share the news with her and we said thank you, together.

As I drove to the office I realized that the commission on this sale was equal to three months of my starvation draw. I had not allowed myself to think that I might actually get the order, but now I was a bundle of emotions.

As I walked from the parking lot to the District Office building I decided to be very calm and professional when I got to the office and quietly say that I'd gotten an order for a six months supply. Instead, when the door closed behind me I shouted, "I GOT THE ORDER!" Ms. Bowes, the secretary, burst into tears and everybody in the office cheered. I turned into Ralph's office and still remember him reaching for my hand while holding the phone to his ear. In doing so, he stretched that phone line so tight that the heavy black receiver was hanging in midair as he shook my hand. Then he threw the phone against the wall, gave me a bear hug and shouted, "Ms. Bowes, we're closing the office and everyone is going down to the bar." It was there that I learned what the order had done for him. It was quite a celebration.

Ralph told me I could go off draw effective the day before and be paid the full commission for this order and all that followed. I accepted and never looked back. In a real sense, I have been on straight commission ever since. Even in the years when I was again on salary I always worked and thought the way I have when on straight commission. This approach to life has served me well.

The mail order company president became a source of referrals for me and the rest of Ralph's team. He told people, "If you want to deal with someone who has your best interest at heart, call this salesman, this company."

My Dad was correct when he said,

"Don't think about your commission. Always think about what is best for the other person, then your wallet will always be full."

Wasn't this a way of showing Customer Care?

Yes, and it is also one of the rules for selling success. The others are:

Listen to your peers and learn from their stories of success and disappointment.

Research before you make the first call. I needed to know the company's payment record and reputation before investing many hours in system design. I also needed to know enough about the business to use their language and terms correctly. This built my confidence and the President's.

Take notes during the call. I do not know who told me to do this but it has served me well. When my prospect also writes notes it is a sure sign I am respected.

Don't back down. Stay the course no matter how much you need the sale in the short term. I remember being very deliberate as I picked things up to leave. I suppose it was instinctive, maybe from watching others, but it conveyed my determination. I was convinced six months was best for the customer.

A Key Insight

In telling you these stories I have embellished them by using the word "educated." The stories are true, but at that time I did not realize that selling and buying are educational processes. This insight did not form in my mind until many years later. It was even later that I learned consulting is also an educational process that uses the same methodology as selling.

The big order put Ralph over the top for his 17th consecutive Club membership and gave me new confidence, but it didn't make Amy and me rich. On straight commission you received half of the commission credit in the month the order was entered and half when product was shipped and invoiced. You received one check a month so I still had to work as steadily and efficiently as possible. I now understood what Dad meant about the law of averages and what Dan meant about 20 calls a week.

The big sale had taught me another lesson. When I looked at my call reports I noted that it had taken no more calls to complete the sale than several much smaller ones had. From that point on I attempted to keep a mix of large and small prospects active at all times.

I now knew enough about my territory to begin calling on larger targets for new business. My first effort, the sale described next, was pivotal to my future success and happiness in sales. Pivotal because of significant insights I gained. I did everything right without trying. In doing so, all I'd learned coalesced and moved me into a new level of professionalism. Have you had a similar experience?

I'm Glad You Called On Me

I had researched this medium size manufacturing company. Its products were large machines with good acceptance in the market. Its sales had grown slowly for three years, while its competitor's sales had grown much faster. It was losing market share for no readily apparent reason.

On my first cold call the Treasurer agreed to give me five minutes of his time. We stood in the hall. I asked him,

"What has made this company successful?"

"High quality, dependable, and durable products."

"You have only two other competitors in the United States. Are they growing as fast as you are?"

"Faster."

I was about to ask why, but hesitated as the expression on his face changed.

"Look, I don't have time to talk now, when can you come back?"

"Next week Tuesday at nine-thirty."

"Can you make it at eight?"

Dan had said, "Ask questions that will make them think about problems they haven't noticed lately."

It was obvious this had happened in this case. I chose the next week because that was my next scheduled time to be in this section of my territory. This was an hour drive from home when traffic was good. I would have to leave home at six thirty to be sure of arriving on time. He had chosen the early hour to fit his schedule and give us time to really explore why they were not keeping up in market share. I allowed two hours for this meeting in planning my calls for that Tuesday and wrote out the questions I would want answered by him.

The call was a complete success. I got my answers. He had been thinking about my questions and his answers since I'd seen him. We were over an hour in conversation before he asked me what I was selling. It was the first time that happened to me and I never forgot its significance. I was so interested in getting information from him I didn't think about telling him what I was selling. We ended the visit with a full plant tour during which I continued to take notes and ask questions based on my furniture and manufacturing plant management experience.

Five weeks and two calls later I placed an order and my pen on his desk. He started to sign it, stopped, searched his appointment book for something that had happened earlier, then looked up at me, and said,

"Six weeks ago I didn't know I had a problem and now I'm buying the solution. You know what inventory is. Most of the salesmen I see don't know what it is when they are standing on it. You are one hell of a salesman, a professional. I'm glad you called on me."

I walked out of there with mixed emotions. I was happy and proud, yet felt modest and thankful. I felt that someone was helping me to help others.

I never forgot that he was glad I'd called on him. Dan had told us that every time we were with a customer we had to deliver value that would make them glad we'd been there, after we were gone. I had done that on every sale I landed before but this time it stuck in my mind.

The installation went smoothly and produced the results the customer had hoped for. The initial order was as large as the nursery sale. I had made a positive difference for both companies.

What was the key to earning this order?

The research before the first cold call!

As the Treasurer told me much later, the receptionist had told him that I had asked for him by name. This made her interrupt him when she knew he was busy and made him curious about me since my name wasn't familiar to him. Then when I knew they only had two competitors in the United States and asked the next question, he felt he could learn from me. My research made this possible.

What other very significant thing happened in this story?

Why do you think it happened?

I did not tell him what I was selling during the first cold call and he had to ask me during the second call. I believe it resulted from several factors.

• Dad's teaching that you always think of what is best for the other person.

- Dan's reinforcement of this with his stress on asking questions to learn about the customer's needs before telling them how you think you can help them.

- The advance research that made me aware that something was holding them back. This focused me on them instead of myself so I forgot to talk about what I sold.

Was I selling, consulting, or both?

Both: I had created a perception of a difference in his mind and made a difference for him by causing him to think about his business differently. This was consulting. As a result, we helped each other and got satisfaction from it. We accomplished all this with tools and methods I sold to him. Those tools had been invented about 20 years before I began selling them. They were a proven and reliable "modern" technology at that time. Today they do not exist.

Speaking Of Technology

We had heard rumors about a new product that we were to sell in this new sales year. It was called a computer. I had read about computers and knew that they were physically big, extremely expensive, computation machines. I wondered how they would fit in our scheme of things and who in my territory would ever use them. The big announcement was made at Club while I was making the sale just described. Everyone at Club had received some education on who would use them and had seen and touched the machine. It was priced at $50,000 or could be leased for $1,100 per month. It had 4,096 words of rotating drum memory in a cabinet the size of an office desk. Most important, a computer sale paid a good commission.

I proceeded to spend free time at night studying everything I could find about computers. The company supplied us with three brochures and something called an instruction manual. It wasn't a very thick manual because this was a truly user-friendly device. There were only 16 commands, which were used to write the instructions, which were called programs. I quickly discovered that the library did not have very many books about computers. In fact, there were so few that I read them all.

It seemed to me that engineers would be the only prospects for the computer. I had no experience calling on engineers and decided to concentrate on selling the "old" technology and look for engineering prospects as a sideline. I had to maintain cash flow. The computer paid a one-time commission even if it was leased and it wasn't big enough to retire on. It turned out to be a wise decision because it enabled me to keep striving for 20 calls a week.

Peer Teamwork Was Key

The end-of-the-day sessions at the bar had given me my first big sale and sent Ralph to Club. They also produced camaraderie and respect that resulted in our helping each other to make Club every year.

It happened that one of my customer companies had a fairly large Engineering Department. I told the Treasurer about our computer first. He was my customer for the existing products and very interested in learning about computers. He became my first student as I learned how to educate people about computers. His questions taught me the questions I should ask to get people thinking

The Perception of a Difference

and excited about computers. He decided the Engineering Department should be using a computer to speed custom order turnaround. He introduced me to the Vice President of Engineering and suggested that he would approve an order for a computer if the Engineering Department decided they could make good use of one.

I found that I had to educate every one of the 20-plus engineers in the department, including those who would probably never actually use the computer. It took several weeks because each person's education had to fit into his/her own workload and into my own selling schedule.

I was two months into my second year with the company and seven months into the first sales year that I was eligible for Club when we decided to take a vacation. On my first day back I arrived at the District Office to hear,

"Congratulations!"

"What for?"

Ralph came out of his office smiling and handed me a copy of the latest company newsletter. My picture was on the front page and the big headline read, "Zimmerman first to make Club."*

"Your computer prospect called the first day of your vacation, asked for a demonstration of the computer, came in with 15 engineers and the Treasurer, who signed an order before they left. I'm taking you to lunch."

---

*Club was a three-day stay in a resort city, all expenses paid. To qualify you had to reach a mandatory sales level or your quota if it was higher. The mandatory level gave you very high earnings and was proof of your sales ability.

This is an example of the wonderful teamwork that Ralph inspired in his district. The salespeople who happened to be in the office that day worked with the fledgling Computer Analyst and successfully did the demonstration. They answered questions and asked questions that educated those engineers and put them at ease. They gave up time from their own selling efforts to do it for me.

All of us were paid a straight, no extras, commission on sales. Any commission split between salespeople was a private arrangement, worked out in Ralph's office. When I first came back from sales class he told me,

"The rule here is that when a bluebird flies in through the open window, we all run to close the window, then we work together to catch the bluebird; after that we talk about how to divide it."

There was no commission split on this, the first computer sale in the district.

I repaid my peers during sessions at the bar where I recounted how I'd educated those engineers, the questions they'd asked, and how I found the answers. Pretty soon other computer sales were happening in the district. It was all a process of education: for us, and the customer.

Loose Lips Saved Me

My third computer sale came about in a way that taught me several lessons.

As I waited in the lobby for my customer two other salespeople, both strangers to me, were talking. It became evident that one represented a company I often competed with, so I looked at a magazine while listening carefully. The competing salesman expected to get an order for a computer from one of my customers: a customer I had received an order from the day before. As soon as I was finished with my appointment I called the next person on my list for the day, rescheduled our time together, and drove 55 miles to the customer who was about to buy a computer.

I told the receptionist that I needed to see John for a few minutes if he could fit me in. He came to the lobby quickly.

"What brings you back today? Did we leave out something yesterday?"

"I just learned that you are about to buy a computer."

"Yes. Is there something wrong with that?"

"I sell a better one than you are about to buy. I've already sold two this year. Why would you buy theirs?"

"Because you've never told me that you also sell a computer."

Three weeks later I had his order. He had been thinking about using a computer since reading my competitor's ad six months earlier. During those six months he and I had been together three times.

I learned two important lessons from the experience.

1. Don't brag or talk about your customers where strangers can hear you.
2. People cannot buy from you until they know you exist and know what products you sell.

This customer knew of my existence but I had failed, in the marketing portion of my work, to tell him about one of my most important products. He could not buy from me until I told him about it. Later you will read a story in which a beautiful robe would not have been purchased if the department manager had not remembered and shown it. It had been on the shelf or rack since the Christmas before last, because no prospective buyer knew it existed. As salespeople we cannot expect the Marketing Department to do the whole job, we must work with them as a team because we need them and they need us.

When you next watch a professional figure skater, horse-rider, or motorcyclist, note how smoothly they move. It is the result of persistence and practice. Each is capable of acting quickly when something unanticipated happens but smooth deliberate actions produce the performance we admire and remember with pleasure. The sales professional also does everything deliberately and smoothly. The results are satisfying for the salesperson and customers. This is what we've seen so far in this book.

In the next chapter we talk about the results when this does not happen.

Chapter 9

Succeeding Without Rushing, Pushing, Shoving

When I began selling as a career, being a salesman was 49th on the list of occupations parents wanted for their sons. The rank rose to 45th during my first 20 years selling. I've seen no new survey results since. I believe I was guided into sales as a calling wherein I could help others. Dad enjoyed selling, as did the several hundred salespeople I worked with through the years. Why then were salespeople ranked so low and rarely considered to be in a profession?

I believe it was and is the result of actions by a small percentage of people in the profession. These salespeople are inept, incompetent, or focused on their own needs. The inept and incompetent lose sales or at worst cause short duration customer aggravation. The inward focus combined with great skill creates long lasting disappointment and anger that is remembered and talked about for years. In this chapter and the next you will see all three in action.

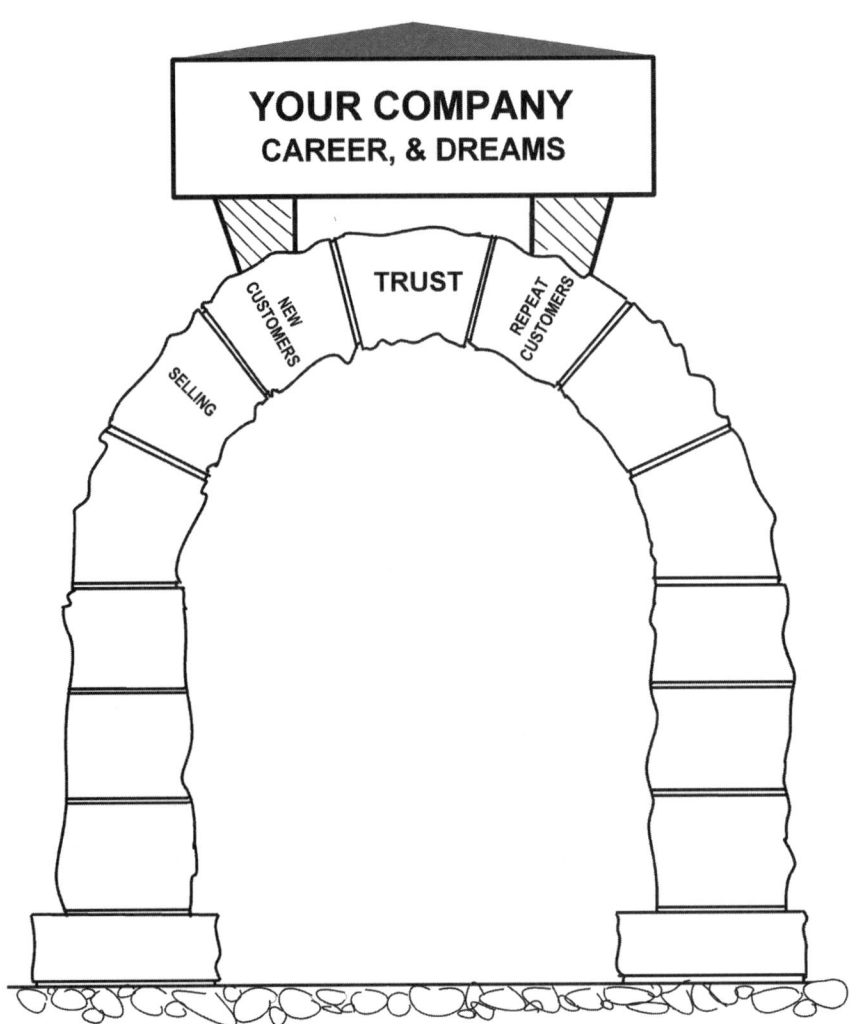

The Business Arch

Listen, Think, Restate, Think, Answer

I attended an all-day seminar on the use of a computer software product that was being used in several thousand installations. Its purpose was to show prospects how the product worked, how easy it was to use, and why it would pay for itself in less than a year. The vendor's marketing and salespeople were the presenters.

The audience ranged from people who were already acquainted with the product to those, like me, who had only read the vendor's product brochure. All of us had a need to know sufficient to warrant giving up a full day away from the office.

The seminar was done extremely well. The product capabilities were presented clearly and in quite enough detail. The day was well paced. I finished alert and awake at 4 p.m. and arose to observe several salespeople at terminals, answering questions while demonstrating to prospects and serious suspects. You know the ones I mean… the ten people out of 50 who had read the brochures, then came to look and were half sold during the seminar.

I listened in on two discussions, then asked the receptionist to call a taxi and joined a third group to learn more while I waited. The salesman was just completing the canned demonstration when I joined the group. He asked for comments.

One person identified herself as Chief Information Officer of her company and asked several specific questions. In each case, she finally got most of the answers from the salesman as part of a lengthy demonstration of several of the product's capabilities. In the give and take, the prospect did a pretty good job of describing her situation — needs, method of operation, etc., — in 30 minutes the salesman never took down a single note on paper.

The prospect was qualified, had the money and authority to buy. She was even in his geographic territory! Then she asked a key, specific question that was very important to her. If the product could do what she was asking, it was obvious (my gut feeling) that she would probably buy.

The salesman gave a simple answer… only not to her question.

She tried again in different words…

He gave her a different answer… only not to her question.

She tried again, this time slowly, at length… drawing diagrams in the air with her finger…

WRONG ANSWER!

I wanted to push the salesman aside and show her how to do it on the keyboard. It's an easy thing with the product — obvious after the day's presentation. It had, in fact, been talked about but the prospect had missed it (so had the salesman). I was so frustrated I couldn't stand it! So was the prospect. She changed the subject, gamely asked the salesman to send her some manuals, and left.

On the way to the hotel, I mentally reviewed the whole episode. I knew the salesman had tried hard. What had he missed — how had he failed?

Then I remembered… Each time the prospect asked her question, the salesman either began to talk before she finished, or he started answering the instant she stopped. He didn't restate her question or his interpretation of what she said, i.e., what he thought he heard her say. His responses indicated that he never heard her questions even though he must have had the knowledge to answer them.

Have you done this in a conversation recently?

If you said no, think about your conversations in the last 24 hours with your spouse or significant other.

What was the salesman doing while the prospect asked a question?

Do you think he got her business later?

The salesman heard the first three words of her question and mentally reached for an answer off the shelf on the assumption that he knew the balance of her question. It is the most common mistake salespeople make. It is the mistake I make all the time with my wife and it aggravates her no end.

Remembering the look on the woman's face and the way she walked when leaving the room I doubt he got the order. His software may have been the best solution for her, but it had competitors. If it had been me, I would have called them and educated myself on their products before making a buying decision.

One last question that you must answer based on your perceptions. I will not give you my thoughts on it:

What level of Customer Care would this salesman deliver?

Why?

Listening And Hearing

Not all of us can pat our head and rub our stomach at the same time. Far fewer of us can "hear" what someone else is saying, while we are thinking about what we are going to say next and what we are going to say after the other person responds. The key to "hearing" is focusing on what they are saying, not just the words but the tone and volume and posture of the speaker as they are spoken. Words, tone, volume, and posture tell you the whole content of the speaker's intended message. Having "heard," the next step is to think about what you heard. If it is a question, reframe it into one that can be answered with a simple yes, to affirm that you and the questioner are in agreement. Then think about the answer before you deliver it. This gives your mind time to catch any errors; then you will deliver the answer with conviction. When you do this, wonderful things happen.

You have credibility.

You are comfortable.

You get the order or continue the happy relationship with your spouse or significant other.

The Perception of a Difference

The salesman in the last story was an incompetent listener. What he and all of us need occasionally is a trusted, observant person to listen to us and tell us what we do right and what we need to correct. Knowing the incorrect things we do is important because we may not be aware of them.

The Gift Of Slowness

The Detroit office developed a system for use in high schools that really saved time in scheduling classes for students. They were selling it very successfully. Ralph arranged for the salesperson who had developed and installed it in several Detroit schools to come to Chicago and teach us all about it. The presentation and discussion was very well done, and I decided to take it to the high schools in my territory.

I set up a sales and installation demonstration for use in the office and landed sales in three schools within a month. I loved it because its advantages to the customer were easy to see and it was easy to install. I became the office expert and helped my peers come up to speed and land sales as well. I did not share in the commissions they earned and did not expect to. It was my way of thanking them for all the help and ideas they were giving me every week.

Ralph observed all of this without comment. One day he asked if I would be willing to travel with him to a branch in Iowa to put on a selling presentation and demo for high school principals. I quickly said yes, even though it would take me away from selling in my territory for three days or more. I knew and liked the branch manager there and knew he would appreciate the help.

During the trip, Ralph and I sat quietly in the train's club car enjoying a cocktail.

"I want you to move and take over the Northwest Branch as manager."

I was totally surprised. I was at the end of my second year with Ralph and was just learning to be a sales professional. I'd been very busy selling and also in my community where I had been asked to run for mayor of our town, campaigned hard, and lost by three votes. Now I wanted to take it easy and sell, because it was fun. All this went through my mind as I looked into my drink while Ralph waited in silence.

"What's happening to the man who's there?"

"He's having some serious personal problems and we have agreed that he should move on to a different kind of work."

"Why me, I'm the least experienced, lowest seniority salesperson in the District?"

"Attitude… attitude… attitude." (He said it slowly, firmly, with conviction.)

"It won't be easy. The repeat business is shaky. Customers have not been serviced well. It is a medium size city with the closeness and culture of a small town. If you lie to one person there, you've lied to them all. You will fit there perfectly. You'll be missed here because you make a difference to everyone. You are respected, you listen and learn and offer help and provide ideas in return. I've watched you put your work for Ms. Bowes underneath everyone else's in her inbox and she promptly pulls it out and puts it on top without you knowing it. Asking you to make this move is an easy decision for me. No one in the District knows about this. Think about it and give me an answer when you've decided."

"Thank you."

He then explained that any commission on sales that I made would be four percent greater than I was currently making and that I would also get four percent of all sales made by my team members. However, the office rent, utilities, and secretarial help would be charged against that commission, so how much I ended up with depended on how good a businessman I was.

"In essence you are running your own business. I have the same arrangement in my position as District Manager."

"In reality, Ralph, that's what I and everyone else in the team is doing."

"Correct."

I sat in silence thinking about it. I noted that he had not mentioned my sales record. We had returned from my first Club attendance a month before and we both knew I was close to qualifying early again: the important thing to him was my attitude.

That night Amy and I talked it over in a long phone conversation and agreed that it was the thing to do. We had only lived where we were for a bit less than two years, but this was an opportunity to grow.

The next day the demo and presentation went well. I felt good and did my best for an audience of over 40 prospects that had responded to the Branch Manager's invitation. There was a lot of give and take with them as they asked questions and I answered them, in what was a teaching session. They were the students. It was great!

Afterward Ralph told the Branch Manager and his team:

"Wes has the gift of slowness. He paused after making each point and allowed everyone to think about it before he went on to the next point. He never answered a question as soon as the asker finished; instead, after a pause, he repeated the question to be certain he understood what was asked, then looked over the heads of the audience while he thought about what he wanted to say. He then answered the question while looking the asker in the eye.

I don't know if you were taught to do this Wes, but I will tell you it is the mark of a professional. Because of those pauses, the listeners will remember more of what you said, for longer, than without them. The approach to answering questions creates great credibility because the perception is that it is a studied answer and therefore can be trusted."

Truth is I wasn't aware that I did this until that moment, but I never forgot it after that. I found I could teach others to do the same thing by getting them to silently count to ten as a pause timing mechanism. Those who practiced this found they could consistently come up with better and more fitting answers than when they did not pause. In later years I came to realize that during the pause the listener's mind was storing the memory location access keys to what was said. This made them quickly available. That's why they remembered what was said and related it to their needs so well.

Ralph and I sat silently for a while in the club car on the trip home:

"I'll take the new position."

"Good, you take over the first of February. Thank you for accepting."

Amy and I looked over the city on our way to celebrate Christmas at my parent's home in Minnesota. On the way there we purchased newspapers and then looked again on the way back.

On my first day back in the District Office, I looked on the bulletin board and read the announcement of my promotion. It was done in Ralph's very simple, matter of fact manner. "On February 1st, Wes Zimmerman takes over the Northwest Branch. Congratulations, Wes." There was a big lump in my throat as Ms. Bowes congratulated me. At the end of the day the whole team celebrated with me as we shared our single drink before driving home.

By the time we were settled in the new office, the Iowa branch manager had received orders from three quarters of the schools that had been represented at my demo and presentation. Most important to him and I was the fact that everyone was a happy customer. Not one was sorry for having made the purchase and changed their scheduling system. This is not always the result of landing a sale.

Buyer's Remorse

He arrived at my home on a big touring motorcycle.

"What happened to the cycle you were riding? You told me it was the third one of that make you had owned."

"Well…I'm not sure now how it happened, but last week I took a long ride into the mountains. After three hours I realized that I hadn't checked oil, filter, etc., before leaving and when I saw a cycle shop sign, I pulled in. It was a small dealership. Forty minutes later I drove out on this monster. Do you know it is so heavy you have to use reverse gear to get out of a parking space? It cost a fortune. The old cycle was paid for. He offered what seemed to be a good deal on trade… I don't know why I bought it.

"On the way back from my ride, I thought about your training session on the buying process and perception of a difference. This dealer has a great POD. I liked and trusted him instantly, so much so that I didn't sense it as he created a faint "want" in my mind and fanned it into a need. He told me about smooth ride, like a Cadillac, and stereo radio, and what a great deal he could give me. I justified it all, Wes."

"Did you take it out for a test drive?"

"Yes, but only in town on the paved streets. After I'd completed the purchase and resumed my planned route I discovered a "Cadillac" cycle doesn't work too well in tight corners on gravel surface back roads. In this state you cannot return a vehicle and get your money back. I wish I could. I guess I'll get used to it."

"You are now suffering Buyer's Remorse."

"Yeah; you told us about that, too."

"Did you feel manipulated by the dealer?"

"No, he was really smooth, enthusiastic, and observant enough to see that I was giving him my full attention and not really thinking about how this big beast would fit in my lifestyle."

"Did you tell him you love to explore the back country and forest access roads?"

"No…and he didn't ask me. He should have known just from the dust on the cycle, and me. He didn't ask any questions other than those needed to do the purchase paper work. He just kept talking about the features of the cycle that made it desirable for his customers. He wasn't interested in me, only in selling the cycle…. Was I manipulated?"

"No, but you did not take time to get a full education and he did not give you a reason to. You acted on impulse, the wild card in at least 50 percent of all buying decisions. He made it work by repeating the features mantra over and over, until you agreed to take a test ride and he kept you on hard paved streets with easy turns, by accompanying you on his own cycle. He may or may not have done this on purpose. What did he ask you to do when you got back to his store?"

"He suggested I move my stuff from my cycle to the fancy saddle bags on this one, while he wrote up the paper work."

"Would you send your friends to him to buy a cycle?"

"Hell, no!"

Dad had said many times; "Always think about what is best for the other person, then your wallet will always be full."

This salesman was highly skilled. He fit the popular image of the "slick" automobile salesman. It is not a complimentary or desirable image, and it is the one that often comes to mind when we hear the word "salesman." This is because the human mind remembers bad experiences and images more easily than good ones. MRI and other medical research tools have shown this to be true.

Do you think this was the salesperson's usual method of operation or did he decide to use it when he first talked to my friend?

My guess is that this person sells this way all the time out of habit. I glean this from the fact that he did not ask any questions to force the buyer to educate him. Salespeople that usually ask questions to help the buyer to educate them, do it out of habit. Manipulative salespeople do not have this habit.

This was a mild form of manipulative selling performed with great skill. It was meant to activate an impulsive decision to buy.

What level of Customer Care would you expect from this salesman?

In your opinion, was the sale completely successful?

If yes: why?

If not: why not?

Now that you have answered the last three questions, jot down who benefited from the sale, long term, and who might have if it had been accomplished differently?

Think about it....

Manipulative Selling

Repeat business and referrals are vital in the long run. This motorcycle dealer will get neither from this customer, worse yet he will get negative referrals for a long time because this customer will tell the story of this purchase for 21 years.* This is the typical result of manipulative selling and the buyer's remorse which almost always follows it.

Manipulative selling, also known as power selling, makes maximum use of techniques to first create interest and then enable the salesperson to, in essence, control the buyer's decision process. I have been trained in, observed, and been subjected to manipulative selling. The successful manipulative salesperson talks fast and continuously without appearing to breathe hard. He knows the applications the product is best suited to, the results of its use, and all the financial aspects of its purchase. He has memorized and practiced the mantra that works best for him.

---

*My Dad talked about a "lemon" automobile purchase for at least 20 years. A research study done in the early 1980s, involving more than 2,400 people, indicated that we remember and talk about a good business experience for up to 18 months and a bad one for as long as 21 years.

The sales mantra is interspersed with questions designed for single word answers with "yes" being the most frequently sought after. Each yes answer is a small decision in favor of buying the product. These small decisions turn the final decision to buy into another small decision. When done smoothly and quickly you, the buyer, aren't aware of what has happened until after the sale is completed. You are in a state of euphoria as you carry the product out the door, or shake hands with the salesperson, or drive down the street in your new vehicle. This wonderful feeling doesn't last if you discover you've purchased the wrong product for your needs or paid too much for something you don't really want. It changes to anger because you feel duped and ashamed of yourself for letting it happen.

This invariably happens when the purchase is the result of incomplete two-way education, and that is the key to manipulative selling. Manipulative selling uses a lot of questions. Those questions are not designed to help the salesperson or you, the buyer, learn what you really want and need. They are designed to move you to a decision to buy before you have time to think about how well the product will satisfy your real needs or how it will impact your cash flow in relation to those needs. The manipulative salesperson doesn't care what your needs are; the intent is to get you to buy before you know if you want to or not.

During the "sales pitch" when you try to regain control of the situation by questioning something, the salesperson treats it as an "objection" and proceeds to overcome it.* This is done by reframing what you said and then changing the mantra so as to regain control of the situation. In a non-manipulative sales discussion there are no "objections."

---

*The terms, "sales pitch" and "slick salesman, slick saleswoman," were invented by people suffering buyer's remorse, looking for a way to save face with friends who asked why they bought something.

The Perception of a Difference

Because I never used manipulative selling, I never felt I had to overcome objections. Many of the sales publications I read spent much time on overcoming objections. Doing so was presented as an essential part of various closing techniques. I ended up buying books written to help salespeople overcome "objections," so I could learn what my problem was.* It literally took me a while to understand why I had never found myself in need of overcoming "objections."

The answer turned out to be simple. I forced the buyer to realize what the real needs were and teach me what they were.** I could then teach him how my product would satisfy his needs, or tell him where to look for a product that would. When I stopped a sales discussion under these circumstances I always received other business from people referred to me by this buyer.

In the business systems sales class, Dan taught us to use questions to speed the buyer's decision process… ethically.

> *"When selling the check writing system, the first step is setting up the demo. While you do this ask how many employees they have. This tells you the quantity of individual payroll ledgers they will need for a year's supply and how long it will take to write payroll with our system. You then do the demo in an unhurried manner. They will note how long it took you to write a check. Then ask the person who usually does payroll to sit down and try it. As they do this, ask what their payroll frequency is and write on your order form the entries for the number of payroll ledgers and checks they will need. Do the multiplication in your head.*

---

*I had the same problem with all the different closing techniques.

**Remember the story, "Six weeks ago I didn't know I had a problem."

"When the person has written two or three checks and feels confident, ask how the speed compares to her present method. The answer will be that it is faster. Then state how long it will take for a full payroll using standard time figures and the number of employees you were given earlier. Ask another person to try the system and while s/he is doing so, hold up the standard check color selection and ask them which color they would like. Mark this on your order blank.

"Answering each of these questions causes them to think positively about the system and sets a yes switch in their mind. Be sure to leave time between questions for them to think, as they watch others use the system. Answer any question anyone asks, when they ask, and do so in an unhurried manner. Get all the information you need while they are using the system. Intersperse these questions with questions about their business, what has made them successful, and who their customers and markets are.

When they complete the demo, hand your order book to the person who can sign and say, "Everything will arrive in three weeks." Then set a time to come in and be with them on the day they write payroll with the new system. If they want time to think about it, accept that answer and set a time to stop in the next time you have scheduled to be in that section of your territory.

"You want them to be glad you came and willing to see you when you come back. On the return visit ask about how they do receivables and wait for them to tell you their decision on payroll. Make certain you give them a useful piece of information or idea on every call. They must get something of value in return for the time they have given you!"

I did not realize until years later that Dan was teaching us to make a positive difference during every call. This created a strong perception of a difference. It never created buyer's remorse. It did create referrals, customers who were loyal friends, and made me an early member of Club year after year.*

The manipulative salesperson does not stop talking, often gets the sale, but rarely gets the second and third one. Manipulative selling may make you a member of Club for a year or two, but you will have to change territories regularly to make it for 15 or 20 years in a row. You will never overcome your reputation as a slick salesperson that can't be trusted.

Ninety Minutes Of Silence

Dan, the brush company District Manager, and every truly successful salesperson I've worked with knew the secret for making customers buy from them the first time and many times thereafter... they knew when to stop talking. With this in mind, compare the modus operandi of the manipulative salesperson to that used in this story. Could you, or have you done something similar?

> We were settled in the new city and had visited with every customer. Business was building nicely. I was attempting to make 20 calls a week and it was beginning to pay off. The phone rang on Friday morning about 8:30.

---

*I missed Club membership twice in my selling career because I got lazy or bored and inconsistent.

"Good morning, Wes here."

"Good morning, my name is Fred Williams with the Water Control Company. Joshua Chval tells me I should talk with you. He says that if you can't help me with my needs, you'll tell me who can. Are you available today?"

"I can be there in 40 minutes."

"Wonderful. I'm looking forward to meeting you."

Fred was several inches taller and 20 years older than I: an imposing handsome man, with a terrific POD. We liked each other instantly. He was Vice President, Engineering, had many patents to his credit, and felt that he and his staff of two engineers needed a computer.

"We don't know anything about computers and are not even certain we can use one, so please enlighten me."

"Tell me what you do that might be better done with a computer. Keep in mind that a computer is a high-speed slide rule (one was lying on his desk) with accuracy far greater than three places to the right of the decimal point."

He described their work and design problems. The new designs were based on historical data going back three decades. The three of them would spend weeks using slide rules to process the data through some fairly complex equations.

"Now that I understand what you are doing, let me show you how you can put it on a computer. Keep in mind that I am not an engineer or a computer programmer, but I can show you how you can put the computer to work on your data."

I pulled a chair alongside of him on his side of the desk and laid out a plain lined pad.

"I'll use this equation (I saw it written on a note pad on his desk). *The instruction set is simple — A is add, S is subtract, M is multiply high order, N is multiply low order, D is divide."*

I proceeded to write the program for his equation, explaining what I was doing as I did it. I could sense him looking down at me thinking, if this salesman can do it I know we can. After ten minutes of this demo…

"I'm sure we can do this. What's the next step?"

"Ideally, we should drive to Chicago and have you spend several hours with our analyst. He is a mathematician, teacher, and programmer. You can bring the equations and data for one of your problems, program it yourself, enter the data, and come back with the answers. Then you'll be able to determine if a computer will make sense here."

"Let's do it!"

"I'll make the arrangements and call you. In the meantime, here is some literature on this computer and on computers in general."

Back at the office I completed the arrangements for the trip the following Thursday, called him, mailed him two additional pieces of literature and a thank you note.

The following Thursday I picked him up at his home and we drove to Chicago — 90 minutes of give and take about him, his career success, his family, and mine. We probably talked about computers and their usefulness for no more than a fourth of the time.

At the District Office I introduced him to our analyst, a wonderful gentleman whose personality perfectly matched Fred's, and left them alone with the computer. Almost six hours later they emerged from the computer area. Fred had a three-inch stack of computer printout in his hands. The cold wind off Lake Michigan hit us as we walked to my car.

"How did it go?"

"Very well. I did all the programming, data entry, everything myself. Phil is a great teacher. He showed me what to do, and why you do it a certain way. After the answers started printing out, he showed me what the computer was doing internally and taught me some programming shortcuts. I've got a lot of thinking to do now."

Those were the last words either of us spoke for the rest of the trip to his house. The sun had set by the time we got in the car, so the 90-minute trip was in the dark. The radio was not turned on. I did not interrupt his thinking. I sensed that was what he wanted. The big car was warm and comfortable; traffic was light. I drove smoothly and safely. When we reached his home I thanked him for his time and we shook hands.

"Have a good weekend."

"Thanks. You, too. I'll call after we digest this computer output and the effort of doing it."

At home Amy and the children were waiting with a late dinner.

"Did you get the sale, Dad?"

"No, he didn't; if he had, he wouldn't be so quiet."

"It was a different, even strange sales call, kids."

I told them about the silent trip home.

"Dad, how did you keep quiet so long?"

"It was the thing to do. Sometimes you have to hear what people say without talking."

I spent Friday at the office, and Saturday and Sunday with Amy and the kids. Monday I confirmed the appointments for Tuesday, Wednesday, and Thursday. I had a full week scheduled. As I was leaving the office the phone rang. It was Fred.

"We've done a lot of thinking and talking about this and we've decided we want to go ahead with the computer. Do you have a contract I need to sign or will a purchase order do?"

"We'll need your signature on a short contract which you can back up with a purchase order."

"Fine. When can you be here?"

"I've got a full schedule of firm appointments through Thursday. Can we do this Friday?"

"Great. Let's say 10:30. We'll get the paper work done, then take you on a plant tour followed by lunch."

Friday was the cap to two great weeks of selling. The signing, the plant tour, and lunch in the company cafeteria were the beginning of a long and happy relationship.

I've been asked; why did you wait until Friday to get the order signed?

At the time I had become so used to planning my time and working my plan that it seemed to be the correct thing to do. I did not want to inconvenience other prospects and customers. It would have reduced the number of calls I could make. It told Fred that I didn't want to waste time, his or mine, and I was confident that they would not change their minds. I realize now that I was sending the message that I trusted them and they could trust me.

Three face-to-face meetings, one with a trusted team member doing the majority of the education, produced an order in exactly two calendar weeks. I think Dan would have been proud of me since the sale to Fred and his team only required three calls out of the 40 that I was aiming for in those two weeks.

The Perception of a Difference

Could this have been done using the phone?

Could this have been done using the Internet and e-mail?

Would a wireless phone have made a difference?

Could it have been done using live videophone technology?

Who besides Phil, the analyst, was on my sales team?

When and how did the power of the perception of a difference come into play?

When did Fred decide whom they would buy from, if they did buy a computer?

At which points in the sale was I the student?

What was the most important thing I did?

What level of Customer Care do you think Fred expected from me?

I ask these questions because technology is always touted as the way to become more efficient and productive. Often our new technology tools become a barrier to real communication. To me this sale is a perfect example of the importance of face-to-face interaction during the buying process.

We needed and used the technology of voice communication.

- Live videophones would have been effective only if the picture was fast without stop and go flicker.

- A wireless phone may have been convenient but would not have changed the result.

- Internet and e-mail would have been slower and would not have conveyed Joshua Chval's satisfaction with my service to Fred in the same way. The interaction in that conversation probably reminded him to tell Fred about my practice of telling a customer who could help them, if I could not. My happy customer was a member of my sales team. After the sale Fred and I both thanked him for what he did.

- Fred used the telephone; I sent a handwritten note in a hand-addressed envelope. The same words in an e-mail message would have had a weaker impact.

- The perception of a difference came into play on the phone in my enthusiastic "I can be there in 40 minutes." It was there also when we met and shook hands. I liked him instantly and could sense that he liked me. Phil strengthened it with a quiet personality that matched Fred's. It was maintained by my approach to getting the contract signed. Mutual trust and respect was the core of this relationship from beginning to end.

- My guess is the decision to buy from me was made between my first visit and the drive to the city. It was strengthened by the relaxed and personal conversation in the car. I did not talk computers beyond the extent he desired. I was the student learning about his personal values and hopes. On the first visit I let him teach me about his work needs.

- It is obvious that I did several important things. I believe the most important one was keeping my mouth shut on the ride back home. What do you think?

This sale made me the first person in the company to qualify for Club in that sales year. It was the second year in a row. Sometimes silence can be golden!

A Management Decision

The textbooks may not say so, but every person who becomes a manager soon learns that managing is all about people and exercising good judgment. Before my promotion I was a hands-on person. My peers and I worked together but we did most things by ourselves. We strove to make personal quotas and did so, landing sales on our own. As a manager I could not do this, I had to depend on everyone else in the team. I had to keep them "up," guide them with suggestions, and learn to feel good when they were successful. If I did this with good judgment they would sometimes "throw me a bone" by asking me to do a job on my own. Invariably it required good judgment.

My team had been working on this sale for almost seven months. I became involved personally, at their request, when everyone below the order signer had been as educated about our proposal as they could be. I was asked to complete the order signer's education and bring in the order. After several visits with him, he asked for time to think it all over and talk with his people. Our only competition at this point was the company whose equipment we would replace if we got the order. This was a big sale and a long, hard-fought sales campaign. If we got it, the sales team that had done the work would go to Club and so would I, the Branch Manager. If not, we would all stay home.

I waited a week for a call from him. Then when I couldn't stand it any more I prepared a two-page letter. In it I listed all the ways our proposal would benefit his company and the follow-up support we would give them. At the end of the letter I asked for the order. I decided to call on him unannounced and hand-deliver it to him.

When I arrived and signed in I saw that our competitor's branch manager and his boss had signed in ahead of me. The receptionist told me to go to the order-signer's office because she thought my competitors had left while she had been away from her desk. When I got to the second floor, they were shaking hands with the order-signer. I could not see their faces but my heart sank because he was smiling. Seeing me, he walked up with a serious look on his face and I died inside.

"I'm glad you came. I just told them that I'm giving you the business."

That letter is still in my pocket. I carry it to remind myself to use good judgment and not to talk too soon.

Opening The Door

Opening the door to the key person's mind is the most difficult part of a sales situation. This is particularly true when the product or service you are selling will impact the lives of many people in the key person's organization or family. The impact will be in the form of change, which no one likes. It can be as simple as changing the color of the company's stationery or as complicated as changing the software program that is used to control order processing and production in a manufacturing plant.

Changing that software will require a change in the work of everyone, with the possible exception of janitors and equipment maintenance people. The person with the authority and pen power to make that buying decision is at or very close to the top of the organization chart. Getting to that person and causing that person to open their mind to new ideas has been illustrated in many of the stories you've just read. The size of those sales and the organizations that bought them were relatively small. In the following stories the opposite was true.

One of my customers told me that I should call on this company. He knew the top man, said that only he could make the buying decision, and warned me that I would have difficulty getting an appointment. He wanted me to get to him because he felt strongly that what I was selling would fill a real need. Of particular interest to me was my customer's belief that the top man hadn't recognized the need, even though he, an outsider, had.

The prospect company was headquartered in a city, six hours by car from my office. I had to get the appointment at a time that would enable me to make other calls in that area on the same trip. I could not spend the trip time and money on that call alone. This meant that I would have to set the appointment by phone. The first time I talked to his administrative assistant she said he was visiting their operation in England. The second time it would fit in my schedule he was on vacation; the third time it was something else. On my fourth attempt he was in but could not speak to me. By this time, his assistant and I had become acquainted and I had won her respect. She told me she would see to it that he called me.

I was in a customer's office when his call came through. I suggested we take a break in our discussions and took the call in a vacant office. His assistant said,

"I told you I'd get him to call you. I told him you wanted an hour of his time."

"Thanks, I really appreciate it."

I had prepared for this but was nervous just the same, his annoyed tone didn't help.

"Why should I give you an hour of my time?"

"You will gain at least one new insight that will help your company, you will get one fact that will help your sales, and you will learn something useful about yourself."

I waited for his next words for what seemed like a long time. His secretary had told him that I could only see him on a specific date two weeks hence and she knew he had no trip planned for that time.

"Can we make it ten instead of nine?"

"Yes, Thank you, I look forward to meeting you."

"You're welcome."

His assistant confirmed the appointment the next day.

A customer had told me that he had gotten those three results from my first visit with him. This was the first time I used them in a situation like this. I had written those items in my planning book so they would be available to see when his call came through. It worked!

The president came to the lobby when the receptionist told him I was there. This was an act of courtesy and showed respect for me. When we were seated in his spacious office,

"Now what do you want to see me about?"

"What has made this company successful?"

"Well…"

He looked surprised then gave me a lengthy answer. Then I asked him the following questions one after another and carefully wrote down his answers.

"What has made you successful?

What three things will do the most to improve the company's sales?

What are your three greatest concerns about the company today?

What are the three biggest problems you face today?"

After answering the last question, he leaned forward…

"I have been talking for 43 minutes and you have been taking notes. I've told you more than I've ever told anyone about this company or myself, now will you please tell me what you are selling and what it will do for me."

"I'm not sure I have anything that will help you. I need time to study these notes and think about your situation. I want to meet with you again three weeks from today. I will then either tell you what I and my company can do for you, or tell you who you should be contacting for help, and why. Until then it doesn't matter what I'm selling."

It was obvious that I wasn't going to stay any longer. I'd used almost an hour of his time and I intended to keep my word. He turned the pages of his planning calendar,

"Can we meet at seven in the morning so we have more time?"

We shook hands and he walked with me to the lobby.

"I'm glad you came. I've learned a lot today. Thank you."

When I got back to my office three days later, I found a note from him.

"You delivered the three things you promised. I'm looking forward to our meeting. Sincerely…."

✧✧✧

I'd done my research and gone prepared with information on his markets and competition. During the conversation I knew what fact to tell him that he did not know. I said nothing about the other two items I'd promised him on the phone. Yet he felt he had received them.

Where or how did he get them?

They were insights he gained from answering my questions. Those questions, which I developed from comments made by prospects and customers, have proven invaluable. The first two are totally disarming. They break down all defenses. They must be asked in a tone that denotes sincere interest and the answers must be listened to in the same manner.

Asking what has made the company successful starts a positive thought process. The person feels good after answering them. This is strengthened while sorting out and expounding on what has made the person successful. That is when he learned something useful about himself.

Asking for three things, improvements, concerns, problems, is key to learning what is really important to the person. The first answer comes quickly because it is obvious and easily taken care of. The second is important and more difficult to accomplish. There is usually a noticeable pause before the person formulates the answer. The third comes only after a period of thought during which the person is deciding if it should be shared with you. It is the toughest to fix, wakes the person up in the middle of the night, and is the one most important to you. If you, your product, or your team is instrumental in taking care of it, you will have a customer for life.

If you say anything between the three answers you will give the person an excuse not to tell you the third item. If you need clarification, ask for it after the third answer is out in the open and written in your notes. Remember, taking notes tells the person that what s/he is saying is important to you. It is a way of showing respect.

Was I serving as a consultant during this call?

Of course! I was getting him to teach me about his wants and needs; as he did so he was gaining insights. The purpose of consulting is helping the client to see problems from a new viewpoint and think about them differently. He'd thought about them a great deal by the time of our next meeting. He was eager to share and compare these new thoughts with the ideas I'd developed.

When your prospect says *can we make it earlier so we have more time*, it is proof that you have delivered value in return for his time.

I developed and began using a Call Plan form fairly early in my selling career. After this experience I made *why should I give you an hour of my time* and the answer I used above an integral part of the form. I use it on all calls for appointments. Using it creates a positive perception of a difference. When planning subsequent calls, I write the three things I want them to learn during the call. The last space on the form has always been;

Why will they be glad I came after I've left?

Writing the answer to this question before I make the call has made me much more effective. This last question, and the one about what they will have learned, fulfills Dan's teaching that the customer must always perceive value received for his/her time.

The Perception of a Difference

Thirty-two Phone Calls

In the last story, opening the key person's mind only required an investment of four phone calls and the effort to get acquainted with the president's assistant. Sometimes a much greater investment may be required.

> One of my personal consulting products is competitive and competitor analysis. This is a service that provides the client with up-to-date information on how his products compare with competing products and how each competitor does business. Ideally, the product analysis includes strengths and weaknesses in different applications and comparisons of suggested selling prices. Most of my clients have also valued price comparisons reflecting discounts, both policy and actual. The client sales force uses the information on competitor sales team selling strategies, and how they vary from time to time. When the information provided is accurate, this service is invaluable to the client's product design, marketing, and salespeople.

Since confidentiality is essential, it is impossible to use references in the effort to acquire new clients. My practice has been to never provide this service to clients who even remotely compete with each other. A great deal of research is done before a company is placed on the list of possible prospects. The final target is selected on the basis of its ability to benefit from our service, ability to pay for the service, and our perceived ability to provide truly accurate information to it. This research had been done for the situation I will now describe.

The next step was learning who in the organization had the responsibility and pen power to commit to a contract. Some of our team talked to people that reported to him, others talked with the target's customers, some of whom had talked with the individual. This gave us a sense of what his reaction to our service would be. Based on this intelligence we decided to prepare a complete package comparing the target's products with its major competitor. The finished bound document contained 75 pages and represented a great deal of effort. I sent this with a single page cover letter to the Vice President of World Wide Marketing and Sales via overnight delivery.

The cover letter stated the date and time of day I would call for his comments. One week later on that date I made the first phone call. His assistant said she would give him a message slip, asking him to return my call. I did this the following day and the next day and the next and… I continued this effort every working day for 31 working days.

In the course of this, his assistant and I developed mutual respect and became friends. She became a solid supporter of mine. During the 31st call, she told me that all the message slips were in one stack on his desk, she had even counted them. I suggested she get a big piece of poster board and tape the messages to it row on row. She laughed, commented that he usually came in quite early, and suggested I use his direct number, which she gave me, to call him before business hours.

The next morning I called him, at six-thirty his time. He answered on the second ring.

"Good Morning. This is Wes Zimmerman, have you read the document I sent…?"

"Yes, from cover to cover, it is amazing. I must assume that the information on XXX is accurate because the information on us is absolutely so. I won't ask where you got our confidential information or XXX's. Are you going to the big conference next week?"

"I've been so busy I've forgotten it, but I'll probably get there for a couple of days because I always do."

"I'm glad to hear you are busy, because that tells me you are successful and I like to work with winners. Will you meet me at our display booth on Tuesday at 10 a.m.?"

"Yes."

"Great!"

That ended the conversation. He'd interrupted my first sentence, talked quite loudly, and was very enthusiastic. I scrambled to make reservations and prepare for the trip.

When I arrived at his company's booth I had nothing with me but my leather bound time planner. I had never seen him or a picture of him, but as I came up to the booth I could tell who was in charge. He saw me, talked to five different individuals, came over, shook hands, and led me to a lounge where it was quiet. He was relaxed, but I sensed excitement under the surface.

I liked him. I expected to discuss our service and answer questions, but never got the chance. The five people he had talked to in the booth joined us. As he made the introductions, I learned that each had a place in his staff. He then announced:

"Wes and his people are going to be working with us for a couple of years. They will help us with marketing, market research, sales education, and a variety of special projects. You've all had a chance to look at the document he sent me. I have written my suggestions on what you should be talking to Wes about (he handed each a slip of paper) *so make arrangements to spend time with him here and back in the office. He will set up a schedule with you today. Wes, I'd like you to come to our hospitality suite at three to meet our CEO."*

Then he left. That afternoon he asked me if I had a fee schedule and proposal for him to approve and put into the system so our invoices would be paid promptly. He did not ask the price and did not look at the proposal while I was with him.

I had been in something of an unbelieving daze all day. I learned we had the order when he told his staff that we would be working together for two years. After that I was busy for over two hours with his staff. I simply could not quite accept the fact we'd gotten the order until after meeting the CEO. Then I called my office where Amy was waiting for news.

"How did it go?"

A big lump rose in my throat and made it hard to talk…

"I guess we've got the business."

"You sound sort of strange, are you OK? What do you mean, 'you guess we've got the business,' don't you know?"

I explained the whole crazy day's happenings. She started to cry, it was one of the largest contracts we'd landed. We had invested a lot of time before I made the first phone call. When I got back home we celebrated.

I learned later that he had scanned the document the day he received it, read it completely that night, and made the decision to use our service at that time. He was very aware of the value of a salesperson's time and would have called me the next day if his decision had been negative. Since it was positive he did not want to call me until he had decided how he would use us. This was his practice and his way of making maximum use of his time. While his staff read the document, he thought of all the benefits that the service would provide, ran a credit check on our company, and sold the whole idea to the CEO. He did not plan on my daily calls, which kept him thinking about it. My early morning call was perfectly timed.

Did we create the perception of a difference and use its power?

Yes, indeed! The document was a complete example of what our service would provide. Our information about his company policies, products, and prices was complete and accurate. He and then his staff were amazed at our ability to unearth information. Our suggestions on the use of it to educate prospects in selling situations provided new insights that would boost sales. The decision to buy was made before he had read half the document. We got his attention by sending it overnight delivery. His assistant did not open the overnight delivery package assuming he was waiting for it. Her perception was that it was important; his was that it was important to us. The cover letter was short with lots of white space designed to say "You can read me in two minutes right now." We wanted him to take it home and read it over the weekend and he did.

The Secret Was Preparation And Persistence.

It took 32 phone calls and almost 200 hours of work just to get him to talk with me. The effort paid off because it opened his mind immediately. He widened the scope of the work while his staff read the document and he got the CEO on board before our first meeting. All of this would normally be accomplished in multiple sales trips to his city over many weeks. In reality, our total cost to acquire this client  was very low. The prospect was ethical, he honored the copyright that was on every page and did not make copies of it until we had a signed agreement approved by both our legal departments; then it became the first deliverable of the contract and was distributed to the people who could put the information to best use.

Let The Other Fellow Sell His

Dad believed that if you can't say something good about another person, you should say nothing at all. He applied this principle in business as well as personal life. One of his sayings was, "I sell my product and let the other fellow sell his." This was his way of never being guilty of disparaging a competitor or a competitor's product.

I remember a story that appeared in a small magazine I subscribed to when I was learning to sell. In it a salesman told of an experience early in his career. He was selling for a manufacturer that was noted for quality, dependable, tough trucks, and highway truck tractors. He had tried several times to get an appointment with the owner/president of a rapidly growing company that used a lot of trucks. When he finally got the appointment, he prepared and practiced what he would say to show how his trucks would truly benefit this company. He never got the opportunity to do it...

"When we had shaken hands he led me to his office, told me to get out my order book while he took a pad out of a desk drawer and said 'I've got a list of the models I want to order from you.' I protested that I had not yet told him about them. His answer was, 'Your competitors have all compared their trucks to yours so thoroughly that they have convinced me yours are the best for me.' He proceeded to give me the quantity of each model that he wanted and his desired delivery dates."

Dad's principle at work: I have never forgotten this story

What the competing truck salespeople probably did was present comparison charts, which is not disparaging. If only one competitor had compared his trucks to this salesman's make it might have worked. It failed when all of his competitors did it, one by one. It failed because they created the perception that the salesman's was the ultimate quality standard they were trying to match. The prospect simply decided the best would be cheapest in the long run.

Dad's principle is sound but, in making a buying decision, you almost have to learn enough to compare competing products. When I attempt to help you in this process and do it in a disparaging manner it can negatively affect your perception of me, and possibly the product I'm selling.

I'm certain Dad knew this but do not remember him talking about it. I did observe that he pushed his own product's strengths in many ways during a sales effort. This was particularly true when he knew the competition had a weakness in the prospect's application. This didn't ensure his success every time, which was painfully illustrated when he lost a major refrigerated warehouse sale. He lost because he would not lower the quality of his specifications so his price would be competitive. He knew doing so would prove disastrous. When the competitor's installation became a disaster, he was asked to come in and do it correctly at his own price. This contributed to his reputation and his high level of referrals.

"No, But..."

When I was selling brushes, the product was of such high quality that all I had to do was make certain the customer used it in the application it was designed for. Selling business systems and particularly the new computers, was a different story.* The typical prospect didn't know anything about the product and was therefore unable to tell truth from fiction. Very often the salesperson wasn't able to, either. I came to the conclusion that to sell effectively I had to know as much about competing products as my own. I acquired that knowledge by subscribing to every industry publication I could find, reading for hours, and creating comparison charts so I would know what to stress to my prospects as I educated them.

---

*Computers were a new technology. Nobody knew what design was best and everyone thought they could design a better one. Consequently, they were different in physical structure and controlling software. I know now that all new technologies go through the same steps on the path to becoming general purpose commodities.

The Perception of a Difference

I had to know which applications my business systems tools and computers could do well and avoid those applications for which they were not suited. When I combined this with knowledge of the applications each competing product was or was not suited for, I began using Dad's selling principle to create happy customers. My customers did not have buyer's remorse, because I made certain they had the best match between application and computer system.

I landed sales by constantly reminding my prospect of my product's strengths in his major applications that were matched by my competition's weaknesses. I presented this in different ways on call after call until one by one competing salespeople would be asked by my prospect, "Does your product have this capability?" The answer would be "No, but…" and the sale would be mine. There is no weaker phrase in a selling situation than "No, but."

You've learned a lot about selling in these four chapters. Your teachers have been pursuers, also known as hunters or outside salespeople. In the chapters that follow your teachers are gardeners, also known as farmers or inside salespeople. In some ways their sales are more challenging because they must complete your buying education in a shorter time. An added challenge for some is that the perception of a difference they create must be strong enough to draw you back to them if you don't buy right away. This is because you often don't or won't give them a means to initiate further contact with you; consequently, they can't correct an error when they make one.

Their stories are just as fascinating as those you've read. You may find them easier to relate to because they involve the sale of items you buy for yourself rather than your business.

Chapter 10

Gardeners And Those That Garden And Pursue

The term inside salesperson appeared in sales literature many years ago. It was used to denote the difference between salespeople who work inside a store waiting for prospects to come to them and salespeople that go to the prospect's location and sell there. The outside salesperson has always pursued business, often doing his own marketing and advertising. The inside salesperson did this only when setting up merchandise displays inside the store and in its windows. The outside salesperson creates business as in "I'm glad you called me" and many of the other stories you've read. Those are the differences.

The selling principles are the same. The educational process is also the same; however, the inside salesperson often has less time for completion because you and I will walk out of the store without setting a time to come back and complete the education.

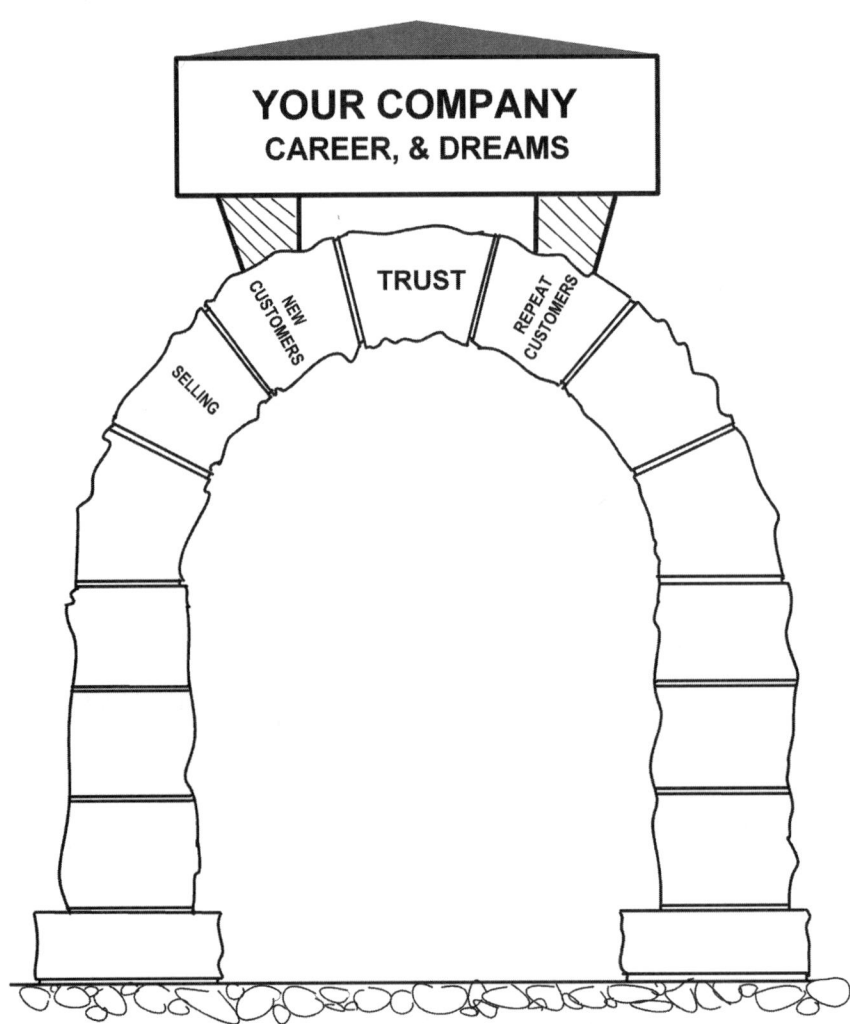

The Business Arch

The professionals in each of these selling situations are rarely successful or personally satisfied if they cross over from one to the other. Those who are comfortable and happy in both, sell products and services that require consultant level professionalism. Real estate sales and business brokering are excellent examples, as is consulting itself. We will talk about and listen to them first.

Real Estate Sales

To sell real estate you do the following things:

- Prepare and execute a marketing plan for your services.

- Acquire a saleable product.

- Package the product.

- Prepare and execute a Product Marketing Plan for it.

- Wait for buyers to contact you.

- Execute the selling process without creating buyer's remorse.

- Create repeat business with ongoing customer care.

Acquiring a product, i.e., listing a property is pure pursuer sales because you must go out and talk to people. Selling a property after listing it usually requires you to wait for the buyer to come to you. The product does not sit on a shelf in the store but the selling approach is identical to selling a product off the shelf. It is inside sales.

Both sides of real estate selling are educational processes. Acquiring the listing requires educating the seller on:

- Your ability and capabilities.

- Your selling approach and why it works.

- The realistic market/sales value of the property.

- The number of months it will take to sell the property in the current market.

- What the seller should do and not do to help the sale of the property.

This is a big educational task and the successful sale of the property *by you* hinges on how completely the sellers accept and implement what you are teaching. In this process the seller of the property is a buyer of you and your services. The perception of your difference perceived in the seller's mind is key. Your POD must win trust and build a strong comfort level. Ideally, it should fit the image of the person they would like to have living in their property. The sellers unconsciously want to sell to someone who will accept and enjoy the property as much as they have. Acquiring a listing is pure selling and the product is you.

Once you have the listing you must package it. Packaging the product includes your advice to the seller on desirable changes that will be cost effective and the way you present the product's strengths in the Multiple Listing Service (MLS) and promotional pieces you prepare. These are marketing and advertising roles that pursuer salespeople have performed for many years.

The most effective packaging will target the most likely buyers for the property. You will have your own perception of who that will be, but do not forget that the seller can help you. No one buys a property they do not like and cannot feel comfortable in, and each of us has different likes. Knowing what the seller likes about the property gives you a clue about what may interest the next owner. Ask the sellers what three things they like about the property. Remember that the third item will be important. If the sellers do not live or work in the property, have each of the people that do tell you the three things they like most about it. Have them tell you this privately or have them write it down silently and anonymously.

Selling the property is an educational process. You must help the buyers to educate you fully on what they want and need. This process begins before you take them to look at available properties. The buyers often will be unable to tell you all the nuances of what they want. On your first face-to-face contact, ask what they liked about the last property they lived in. Have each person write down the three things they liked most. When you read their answers and compare them to what sellers have liked in properties you've listed, you will know which properties to show first.

You continue to learn as you accompany the buyers when they look at properties. Listen, guide, don't talk, but watch their eyes, body language, where they pause to look and think. Note these things mentally; write them down if at all possible. Don't talk except to answer their questions and where needed, to draw their attention to items on the list of things they liked in past home(s). After each visit ask "What did you like about this property?" Write down what they say, noting the manner, tone of voice, and "feeling" as they speak. You will then know where each "like" falls in their priority list.

This written record is essential to your success. It enables you to build a list of all the things they like which you use in research on the multiple-listing system. The process makes them feel good because you are showing them properties with a high probability of pleasing them while making maximum use of their time and yours. This strengthens their positive perception of your difference and makes them want you to be their agent even when they decide on a property being shown by a different agent.

Always protect your perception of a difference and be careful that others on your team also protect it. As the next story shows, choose your companions carefully.

If She Marries Him...

The real estate agent we had worked with when we built the home we'd lived in for 20 years called to ask if she could visit. My wife and I looked forward to seeing her and were pleased she was still interested in us. She had been most helpful. She brought her fiancé with her. She explained that her husband had died several years ago and that now she wanted someone to work with her in selling real estate. Her fiancé had been a general contractor and builder of homes. She knew I had actively monitored the building of the house and wanted to know how things had turned out. In the conversation, I mentioned that I had asked for extra heavy wire in the outlet circuits and cited it as an example of the quality built into the house. To my amazement, her fiancé immediately took a screwdriver from his pocket, opened an outlet, examined the wire in it, and announced that it was not extra heavy.

I felt like a fool and was very embarrassed. All I wanted them to do was leave as quickly as they could. It was obvious the realtor was embarrassed, also. When they were safely out of the house, my wife said,

"If she marries him she loses our future business and recommendations."

"Honey, I could not believe it. I wasn't aware that the electricians had not followed my instructions. This was not the time or manner to find out."

Openly questioning the veracity and intelligence of a seller just won't work in real estate sales. This incident probably killed the relationship because a few months later the realtor came by to renew acquaintances and remarked that she had broken the engagement. We did not mention our embarrassment.

We Learned By Moving

We started life together in Illinois where we built the first home we owned with our own hands and the help of friends on weekends. It was a tremendous experience and used everything I had learned on the farm and working in Dad's business. The house was so tight the building inspector would not allow us to move in until we installed a permanent fresh air inlet in the furnace area. At 710 square feet it was the smallest house we would ever live in.

We went on to buy and sell a total of eight homes in three states, which gave us a lot of experience with real estate salespeople. Though we had not developed the insight of the perception of a difference, we quickly learned to never do business with a real estate agent who caused our "livers to quiver" on first contact. Looking back on our experience I realize that every house we bought and later sold was handled by the salesperson that was most informative and consistent in listening and doing what was promised when it was promised.

Janet stands out in memory. A member of the Kiwanis Club I had joined recommended her. She was a veteran in real estate sales. She insisted on coming to the rented house we were living in and visited for quite some time. She was observant of how we had set up the house, what our children were like, and the things we enjoyed doing as a family. She looked at every room and the basement during this process. She asked enough questions to learn what we liked about the house and why we had chosen to rent it in preference to others we had looked at. Then she went away. Today I would say she had a great POD. We were completely comfortable with her.

About two weeks later, as she had promised, she picked me up at my office and drove me to look at three houses from the street. In each case she drove slowly through the neighborhood, pointed out available shopping and the distance from the house to it, and showed me the school our children would attend. When this tour was over I knew which house my wife would like.

Janet made arrangements for us to see it with her in leisurely fashion and we bought it. We bought it because it had all the things we liked, including a small but lovely backyard with two perfectly formed evergreen trees and a sun room ideal for indoor flowers in pots; important to us because this area had long cold winters. There is no question that the tall pine and the magnificent blue spruce had a great deal to do with our buying decision. We loved and lived in that house almost five years.

She landed the sale in three visits, over a three-week time period.

How did she do it?

She had salt and pepper hair; had been selling there for over 25 years and had sold each of the houses she showed me two or more times before. She had a record of what each buyer and seller had liked about each house. She must have compared what she'd learned in her long visit with us to those records, then taken me to the three she felt would most appeal to us. The time she took to record that information after each sale saved a great deal of time later.

What else was significant about her?

Historically, the average ownership of a home in that area, at that time, was seven years. She had sold each of the homes two or more times. This means she had kept in touch with the owners and serviced them in various ways so well they listed with her when it came time to move. This was significant to me in this story. She never created buyer's remorse. She kept her customers happy over an average period of seven years. This reduced her time and effort in listing properties and with her records, shortened the time to find buyers. Wow!

Go thou and do likewise.

✧✧✧

Always Ask What They Like

The client's major business was managing rental properties for investors and caring for vacation homes in a seasonal recreation area when owners were living elsewhere. This business was augmented by a six-person real estate group. I had executed a complete program on the perception of a difference with the usual result of better customer service and a renewed team spirit in the property management group. The real estate group attended those workshops appropriate to their work; now on my last day they asked if they could talk with me for a couple of hours after lunch. I had no idea what they wanted and was a bit concerned about my ability to meet their needs whatever they might be. We sat at the conference table so they could write notes on what I said.

"What do you want of me?"

"We've put into practice what you've taught us in the workshops, over your last three quarterly visits, with good results. We are happy about it, but we are hoping you can give us something special that will increase our sales success."

I sat in silence…. I did not know what to say… so I silently prayed for help.

"I don't know of anything special. I am not a real estate expert, but I'll tell you about our experience buying and selling houses."

As I did this I remembered the Janet story and saw the similarity to the buying experiences we had liked best. Then I knew what to tell them.

"What do you ask your prospects when you are showing them a house?"

"We first try to find out what they particularly hope for, but up here every house has at least one fireplace and a beautiful view, so all we can do is show them houses within their budget. We end up spending a lot of time showing houses."

"What do you ask them when the showing of each house is over?

"What don't you like about this place? Then we try to take them to a place without these items."

"And you build up a list of things they don't like."

"Precisely."

I told them about Janet and how she took care of her buyers.

"We don't have the luxury of time that she had. Our prospects come here for a weekend for the purpose of finding a vacation home and enjoying the surroundings. They don't want to take the time to sit down and discuss anything."

"Then ask them what they like about each place and build up a list of likes. In the process you move them from negative to positive thinking. When you do this make sure they know it's OK to say they like the tree in the back yard."

They laughed.

"Then you will be doing exactly what Janet did, only in a different way. Always ask what they like. Let me know if it helps your sales, please."

Six weeks later the head of the group called.

"It works! It works so well our sales as a group are up 20 percent and climbing. We found out that asking what they don't like was a habit and it took some of us longer to build the new habit than others. That's why sales are still climbing for the group as a whole. It's much more fun to think about things that people like than things they don't like. Believe it or not, one couple bought because of the tree in the back yard that reminded them of a place they lived years ago. We laughed about it and wanted you to know."

✧✧✧

Because the human mind remembers or at least accesses unpleasant things easier than pleasant ones, it is easy to remember what we didn't like. When I ask you as a buyer to tell me things you like as you leave a house, I cause your mind to imprint that in an easily accessed area. My experience is this puts you in a positive, feel-good mood, and at the next house you look for things you like and compare them to the things you liked at the last house. If I write down what you liked at each house it is easy for me to think of other places that have things similar to your likes. I end up with a positive outlook and the whole day goes better for both of us.

Business Brokers Succeed The Same Way

I have never sold a business either as a seller or as a broker but I have talked with and consulted to Business Brokers. This is what one told me.

> I sell small to medium size manufacturing companies. Many are family enterprises founded by the present owners or their parents. They are complete operations with design, marketing, and salespeople. They employ as few as 25 to as many as 300 people. These people have made the business successful or turned it into a loser for the owners. Owners are usually active in the company on a day-to-day basis.

> I market my services with direct mail addressed to the principals by name with envelopes marked confidential and through attendance at appropriate conferences. I may have a booth at a conference or just network with people and hand out brochures. It is rare for anyone to tell me they are considering selling on these occasions, but as a result of these efforts I receive phone calls. Then the work begins.

> I do a lot of research about the company: its financial history, its employee relations history, its customers, and how happy they are. I need to know the market position of its products currently and in the next five years. I need to know the strengths of management individuals, both those that will leave and those who want to stay after the sale. I put all of this information in a bound marketing presentation for use by qualified, serious potential buyers.

> Then I send a very discrete mailing to the list of potential buyers that I have built up. Some of these are people who have contacted me stating what type of company they would be interested in should

it become available. I call these personally. I also place advertisements in appropriate periodicals. After that I wait for the phone to ring. Ideally, I want several companies at different points in this process at the same time: like products on the shelf.

When a potential buyer calls I do research on them, also. The financial muscle and management ability are of prime importance. I need to know if they will have a positive or negative impact on the employees of the company they buy. If negative and many employees leave, the company loses value and customers, and may even fail. When you buy a company, you are buying people and their knowledge that makes the company run.

My buyers seldom pay outright for a business. They pay for it out of the earnings of the company during the first three to five years after the sale. The current management usually agrees to stay on during this period to ensure success in the transition. So they and the new management must develop mutual respect and be able to work together. Payment for the company is in installments tied to earnings. Each sale is a long educational process in which I am consultant, teacher, mediator, and sometimes contract negotiator.

I am most often contracted as the seller's representative. What I've described is that situation. If a buyer or investor group contracts me to find a suitable company for their purchase, I do the same research and education.

In either case, the buyer and seller do their own due diligence and make their own decisions. My responsibility is to make certain my research is as complete and accurate as I can reasonably make it. Because the sale of a company invariably includes real estate, I must be licensed as a Real Estate Broker or work through a licensed Broker in the state(s) in which the property is located.

This man is a professional at the consultant and counselor level of sales. He wears a suit and tie most of the time but sometimes dresses down to match the dress of the seller or buyer. His success is based on trustworthiness. On first contact my perception was that he was habitually cautious and could be trusted. Longer contact with him proved this to be correct. He also is very deliberate and outwardly unhurried in everything he does. He has been very successful in his business.

Note that his selling uses the same principles as every other salesperson we have listened to; only the details are different.

Gardening... Pure Inside Sales

We've listened to Gardeners that also pursue. Now we'll talk with pure inside salespeople. They are true professionals, yet are often held in low esteem by the customers they serve so well. You will see why in the story *"The keys slid under the car."*

If you are a gardener salesperson you will see yourself in more than one of the following stories. If you are a pursuer with the perception that pursuers are superior to gardeners. you will see everything you do, illustrated by gardeners who cannot regulate their opportunities by planning their time and making appointments. They must make their sales without being perceived as manipulative. It's a different, maybe tougher situation. Think about it....

This Will Look Good Right Here

The car I used for my business travel also served for all family outings and vacation trips. I maintained it carefully and never experienced any problems with it. On my way to the office one day, I noted that the odometer read 167,000 miles and on impulse decided to pull into a dealer franchise and look at a possible replacement. I went into the dealer store, looked at the single auto in the showroom, then walked up to a very large wall chart loaded with information about this make's various models. No one had greeted me when I came in. In fact, I wasn't aware that anyone was in sight of the door. Now a gentleman was quietly standing beside me.

"How many miles do you drive a year?"

"22,000."

"In sales, over the road for long trips?"

"Yes."

"How many children do you have and how old is the oldest?"

"Four; oldest is thirteen."

"Do they travel with you on vacations?"

"Yes."

He handed me his card and I gave him mine.

"Mr. Zimmerman, you should consider a station wagon. Ours is very stylish, has a lot of class, rides and handles like a luxury automobile. Three seats will provide room for the whole family without crowding and arguing. Let me show you why it will give you the comfort and quiet you need on your sales trips."

He proceeded to explain all the features described on that wall chart. He did not have a station wagon in stock at that time. He took me out to the service department and introduced me to the service manager. He requested that a new car be brought in off the lot and put on the lift. He showed me the undercarriage and why it delivered comfort and quiet transportation.

The service manager explained his philosophy of customer care and pointed out the completeness of the shop's equipment. I was impressed by the cleanliness of the shop, the professional manner and dress of the service manager, and the fact that the salesman's jacket and pants matched. He was wearing a business suit, which was not the usual attire for an automobile salesperson. Above all, he got me involved enough that I took a package of information back to the office with me.

Three days later he called to invite me to bring my wife and drive a station wagon that had arrived. He directed me to drive on the highway as well as in the city. About a third of the way through the route, he asked me to stop and asked us both to get out to look at a feature under the hood. When we got back into the vehicle we were much more relaxed and I was more confident driving it. He answered every question with courtesy and respect. He made no effort to push us to a decision that day, nor had he on my first visit. We went home with more literature and the notes we had taken while with him. The children got into the act, and our oldest son skillfully helped his three siblings to decide the single, rear-facing third seat was better than the two that faced each other.

A few days later I signed the order for our specific combination of color, upholstery, and other options along with a check for ten percent of the agreed price. During the two weeks between my first visit and last, I visited two other dealership stores. One sold the same make; the other sold a competing make. In both cases I was turned off by the manner in which I was treated and talked to. Subconsciously, I compared this to the way I was treated at the first store. Above all, these people attempted to rush me into a decision, which I resented. I was already successful as a salesman and manager of salespeople and found myself telling Amy what these salespeople were doing wrong.

We were completely comfortable with our decision to buy from the first salesman. He was professional in appearance, manners, and language. He never talked down to either of us.

He called us when the station wagon had arrived and made arrangements to have us picked up and brought to the store. When we were seated in the car, ready to drive away, he handed Amy an envelope, reached in, placed his finger on the dash and said,

"This will look good right here."

As I drove away Amy opened the envelope and found a metal plate of the right color for the car, engraved with the words, *Wes & Amy Zimmerman.* Double sided tape to install it was also in the envelope. That nameplate was still on the dash seven years later.

✧✧✧

Was he a professional?

Did he make me educate him about my needs?

Do you think that I would have told him what he needed to know without his help?

Did he educate me? Amy?

Did he earn our trust?

Did the perception of a difference play a role in his success with us?

Did he have a partner in the sale and did he use that partner effectively?

Did he communicate the level of Customer Care we would receive?

I was 38 and Amy 34 at the time, yet, even at that young age, respect played a major role in our perception of his positive difference. His quiet, unhurried approach with us was the exact opposite of manipulative selling. It communicated respect and his confidence. It caused me to lower my defenses, answer his questions, and enjoy the process of buying an expensive automobile. The service department manager, his partner in the sale, exhibited the same approach, which made me confident they could and would provide any service I might need later.*

---

*The engine quickly began to use oil excessively. This grew worse as the mileage grew. When 500 miles remained on the warranty and a quart of oil lasted 175 miles, the service manager made the decision to open the engine. The oil rings had been installed upside down on the pistons. They gave me free oil changes for a time to pay for the excessive oil consumption. After the ring problem was corrected oil consumption was normal for 100,000 miles.

The salesman was there to greet me every time I brought the car in for service. He checked the service department appointment book daily in order to know when one of his customers was to be there. This was his equivalent of the customer service calls that Dan taught us to do in sales class. It worked; we urged everyone we knew to buy their next car from him.

He did everything a pursuer salesperson does, except pursue!

What Size Does She Wear?

On our wedding day, which was also her birthday, it was very warm for February. Now on this anniversary morning it was very cold. I had gone to sleep last night realizing that I had no birthday gift for her… not good… not good. The first step was to get the fireplace blazing brightly before she came downstairs. Second step was preparing a mug of hot chocolate. As she accepted it she shivered.

"I need a long, warm robe!"

Voila! That will be her birthday gift. I quickly came up with an errand that had to be done before noon and "won't take long." I was the first person in the door when the department store opened, asked where ladies robes were and went directly there. The only person in the area was a woman.

"Good morning. What can I find for you?"

"It's my wife's birthday, I forgot to get a gift, and she needs a long, warm robe."

"What size is she?"

"Your height, build, and lovely figure, a lady with class.

"Thank you."

She thought a minute, then went directly to a rack, came back and put on a robe she had remembered. It was thick, sort of quilted in a fine pattern, white on white, and just beautiful. I knew enough about women's clothing to know it was a designer: one of a kind, and expensive. I knew my lady would love it. It was what she would select if cost were not a concern.

"It's beautiful! It brings out your beauty; it will hers, too, and I'm certain I can't afford it."

She reached into the pocket of the robe and looked at the price tag, which I could not see.

"I'm the manager of the women's department. This robe has been here since Christmas two years ago. Do you have thirty dollars?"

"Yes."

"I'll gift wrap it for you."

"Thank you very much."

She made me educate her with her questions. She thought about my need and solutions to my cash problem. She educated me on why and how it would fill my need by putting it on. Then she made a key decision, landed the sale, and made me very happy. All this happened in less time than it took to gift-wrap the robe. Everything a pursuer salesperson would do. She was a professional.

Why do you think she quoted such a low price?

Do you think my education of her influenced her decision?

My wife loved the robe; still has it 40 years later.

The Chair You Always Wanted...

My wife called my office an hour before lunch with great excitement in her voice.

"On the second floor of XXX, in the furniture department, there is a green leather chair exactly like you have always wanted. Please go and look at it when you go out for lunch."

I spotted it right where she had said it would be. A handsome design that begged to be relaxed in. The color was the perfect green, not too dark, not too light, or too blue or yellow. From past experience I knew what to look for in construction and craftsmanship. It communicated quality. I sat down in, not on it, leaned back, opened my overcoat, tipped my hat down over my eyes, and instantly fell asleep. Thirty minutes or so later, I opened my eyes.

"It fits you well now and it will shape itself to you over time, so much so that you won't let anyone else sit in it."

"I did not expect to fall asleep when I sat down."

"I watched you from a distance. I knew you would like it."

He was sitting about three feet away where he could watch me. He was a professional; gray was showing at his temples. He had the wisdom to let me sleep and steer people around me while motioning to them to be quiet. He told me this as I walked around the chair twice looking at it and picturing it in our house where my wife had told me it would fit. I remember that I did not look at the price tag.

"Put it on our account and deliver it this week, please."

I think of this professional salesman and the entire incident at least once a week when I sit in it. It fits me so well that I have difficulty staying awake in it and if I close my eyes I'm off to dreamland. I educated him by falling asleep in it. He educated me about what to expect from it with use.*

---

*The chair does fit me precisely because leather stretches and molds and the seat and back cushions are filled with rubberized hair from the tails of horses, a material no longer available. Modern plastic foam does not have this wonderful capability. Alas, it never molds itself to anyone.

I Wear Size 10D

I was on a sales trip when I realized that my shoes looked terrible even after being polished. I walked to a shoe store following the directions the hotel desk person gave me.

"I need a black wing tip in size 10D."

"Please sit here so I can measure your feet."

"I don't have much time and I wear size 10D."

"Either I measure your feet or you go somewhere else for shoes."

"I haven't time to go somewhere else."

"Your left foot is a tad bigger than the right one and has a higher arch. Ten and one-half E is the correct size. You have gained weight since you were young and some of it is in your feet, also. This is why the sides of your shoes are bulged over the welt, (he picked one up to show me) *and your big toes wear out the toes of your stockings prematurely. A style with a higher toe profile will help your comfort, also. I'll be right back."*

He brought one pair. They fit perfectly and were very comfortable.

"Why hasn't someone told me this before?"

"Either they didn't know any better or you were impatient and they didn't want to risk losing a sale by taking the time to tell you. My partner and I have been selling shoes for 20 years and we know most men and women wear shoes that are too small. This provides business for foot doctors. I'm betting the next time you need shoes you'll try to arrange your travel plans so you can buy them here."

I did… twice.

If this reminds you of *He was blocking the door* it should. His tone left no doubt in my mind that I would either let him measure both feet or walk out in my old shoes. He educated me fully. He proved his point by showing me the bulged sides of my shoes and I knew the toes of my stockings got holes sooner than the heels. He earned my respect and confidence.

He was a professional at the consultant level for sure.

Look, It's My Watch!

On a walk through softly falling snow we stopped to look in the jewelry store window. We would walk away from the altar a month later, wearing rings this jeweler had given me in exchange for painting the store interior after hours. It was the only way I could afford them. We came by to admire my work through the window and look at his display. Then she saw the wonderfully small, unique, wrist watch. Solid gold rectangular case with a prismatic glass face and black cord band, strikingly beautiful; its price would buy three of our ring sets.

"Someday I'll buy it for you."

Six years later we were in Fort Wayne, Indiana, with another couple. We had driven 100 miles to shop and eat at a fine restaurant. We parked and started walking. Our route took us past the city's finest and most expensive jewelry store.

"Let's go in and look around."

"Sounds like a great idea."

On entering we found the store had display cases around the perimeter with salespeople stationed at intervals in back of them ready to talk to prospects. Amy led the way and turned to the case immediately on our right; I followed. She had gone no more than four feet when she stopped.

"It's my watch! Look, it's the watch we saw in the window the month before our wedding."

I watched as the white-haired gentleman took it out of the case and put it gently on her wrist. It was the perfect size for her wrist and hand and it had class to match her own. She told our friends the story of when we had first seen it. She did not see the moment when the gentleman and I made eye contact as I joined in the conversation with her and our friends.

"You promised that you'd get it for me someday."

"Yes, I did, but the price is higher now than it was then and we don't have the money. We don't even have the money for a down payment."

"You've got ten dollars you said you brought just in case we needed it."

"Yes, I've got ten dollars and I could pay ten dollars a month until it was paid for, but you have other things you want."

"Promise you'll get it for me next year?'

"I promise."

By this time we were halfway around the perimeter of the store. The gentleman was walking with us, offering to take items out of the case for the women to look at. He listened to every word; we were not whispering. I laid my business card face down on the case at the midpoint of our trip around and noted that it disappeared quickly. When we reached the door Amy was the first out and I was last. The gentleman shook my hand with his card palmed so I would get it. Not a word passed between us. No one had seen the exchange of cards. When I could read his privately; there was one hand printed word on the back, "WHAD." When I returned to my office I sent him a $10 bill with a thank-you note.

Nine months and nine payments later, I drove the 100 miles with the balance and picked up the watch.

"I didn't know what else to put on the card lest it be understood if your wife found it. When I received the first payment I knew you understood."

*"Of course! It said, "**W**e **H**ave **A** **D**eal."*

I put the watch on a branch of the Christmas tree where it reflected the light from the tree lights. When we came back from Christmas Eve church service and the kids were in bed, I turned on the tree lights, left the rest of the room dark, and waited. She walked around the tree admiring the ornaments and then started crying…. She had found the watch.

Another professional making a decision on the fly: the salesman was observant and heard me as I talked with Amy and educated him on what was needed to make the deal and the happiness that would result. I've often wondered if I would have thought of "WHAD."

They All Disappeared

The convertible was one of 5,600 that had been built 18 years earlier. It was, and still is, a large impressive car with a mighty V8 engine. It went directly from the factory to the dry air of the Phoenix, Arizona, desert so rust was no problem, but the paint was faded and it needed new upholstery. I was considering restoring it to its original glory and was researching the cost. On this day I was dressed in grubby clothes instead of my usual tailored suit and tie. I had been told that this Cadillac dealer's body shop was the best place to get the new paint job, but I was having a lot of trouble finding it. I decided to go into the new car showroom and ask for directions to the body shop.

I swung into a parking space directly in front of the showroom. As I did, I saw at least six salespeople in suit and tie, looking at me through the window. I got out of the car and headed for the door… suddenly there were no people in the showroom window. When I opened the door I saw the back of one person disappearing through a door on the far side of the room. I looked around for someone to give me directions. The place was empty.

I looked at each of the cars on display, comparing them to the Lincoln Towne Car I normally drove. When no one showed up and the reception desk remained empty, I headed for the door. On the way I saw my reflection in the showroom window and suddenly understood why I was alone. My appearance and the run down appearance of the old convertible had created a perception of a difference that did not measure up to a Cadillac automobile. When I traded the old Towne Car for a new one a year later, I did not bother to check out a comparable new Cadillac even though the price was essentially equal.

Professionals can be snobby and arrogant.

The moral is: Judge not lest ye be judged.

They Slid Under The Car

My client was the Vice President responsible for Marketing, and a professional sales force with offices in cities across the country. When he came to our meeting I could see he was agitated. He indicated he wanted to get something off his chest before we talked about our project.

My family has been blue-collar as far back as we can trace our ancestry. I am a part of the third generation born in America, and I am the first one to graduate from high school. Getting a college diploma with honors and being successful makes me a person to emulate in my extended family. I find this humbling and a great responsibility. It has also made me aware of how important it is to treat others honorably and with respect, the way they have always treated each other and me. Today, I was reminded of this again.

The Mercedes has a lot of miles and I've been thinking that since American cars are once again well made, my next one should be American. It would make the family feel good if I buy a car built of the steel they have produced in the mills, so I stopped at a Cadillac dealer store on my way here. I entered the showroom behind an older couple. It was apparent that there was only one salesperson on duty and I was second in line, but today I only wanted to look at and sit in one of the cars.

The salesman was wearing a suit, the older gentleman was wearing a suit and I'm wearing a suit. The salesman knew I'm driving a Mercedes. He greeted the couple, looked at me, and said,

"What can I do for you, buddy?"

"Today I just want to look at that white, four-door sitting in the lot over there and get a feel for it."

"OK, I have to take care of these people first, but if you'll go out and look at it I'll get the keys for you in a minute."

I went out to the car, which was parked in a muddy puddle from the rain last night. Then I heard,

"Hey, buddy, (I looked up at the salesman) *here's the keys.*"

He threw them at me and they slid under the car into the mud puddle. I left them there and drove away.

If he were one of my salespeople, I'd fire him! I am not his "buddy."

If he could not handle two prospects at once he could have asked me to come back at another time. Buying an American car doesn't seem so important any more.

Have you had a similar experience?

What was your reaction?

✧✧✧

Dress Me

When I worked in New York City I had the privilege of working with a classy woman. She was a very effective sales professional who always was perfectly dressed. One day she came to the office in a completely new outfit that complimented her complexion, skin color, and figure. It was feminine without distracting your thoughts from what she was saying. It was the perfect business attire for this woman. I was curious as to how she achieved this.

"How many times have you gone shopping to put this new outfit together?"

"Once, plus trying it on for final fit, when I picked it up."

"You mean one day and stops at several stores?"

"No. I've been going to the same women's wear shop and the same man for years. I walk in and tell him, dress me for the office, or dress me for a dinner party; then I stand still and let him do his thing. I rarely have to tell him I don't like something."

"He is a professional."

"Yes, he has a complete record of my measurements and what each outfit I've purchased consists of: color, style, sleeve and skirt length, accessories, everything. He explains the reasons for his choices and the situations in which they will work best. He makes shopping fun, easy, and quick."

The Perception of a Difference

She and this professional's other customers keep coming back because of the service he provides. He is not a low-priced source for women's clothing. He has combined a special talent for clothing with detailed record keeping about his customers and their purchases to create a perception of a difference.

Is it worth it?

You should see his stock portfolio.

Pursuing Or Gardening, The Process Is Education

The difference is how you, the seller, and I, the buyer, first come into contact and how long it takes. When I come into your store I have usually completed the first two steps in the buying process or I am in the second step. This is not necessarily the case when you come to my place of business. In both cases, our meeting is the beginning of an iterative process, in which you ask questions to help me to teach you, and I ask questions to help you teach me.

Whether you come to me at my place of business or I come to your store, you must assume I am going to buy what you sell *from someone* if it *fits my needs,* as I perceive them. To earn (not win) my order you need to learn what I perceive my needs to be in terms of *end results* and then teach me what I need to know so that *I* can decide *for myself,* what will best produce those results.

Look at the items in italic… what do they tell you?

You cannot use a shotgun, boilerplate, or manipulative pitch, without running the risk that I will buy from someone else or have buyer's remorse if I buy from you. You must get personal and specific information from me, to teach me what I need to know. I won't give you that until I like and trust you.

Start by creating a positive perception of a difference, in my mind. Here are some things to remember.

I am like the birds sitting in a row on a wire; I do not want you invading my space. Being too familiar, too soon, is a way of invading my space. So is standing too close to me. If you do I will become defensive and look for an exit.

Do not call me "buddy," "man," "pal," "honey," "sweetie," "dear," "hon," "handsome," "lady," "beautiful," "girl," "chum," "doll," "bud," "fella," "sunshine," because all of these tell me that you are lazy and do not consider me equal to you.

No matter what my age, call me Mr. or Ms. and use my last name until I tell you otherwise. Until you know my last name, call me Sir or Madam or Ms. Do this because I want and need respect. When you show me respect, I will show respect to you in return. If I do not, break off the conversation, make some excuse to leave and forget about selling me anything. If I buy from you without respecting you, I will probably blame you for every problem I have with the product.

The man from the blue-collar family didn't buy because he was not shown respect. I remember a man who put his feet on his desk while we talked. He was not showing me respect. I wasted my time making a second call on him, but thereafter I did not allow anyone else that opportunity; neither should you if I am the buyer.

If I come to your store the same rules apply. If I do not show respect for you, please excuse yourself and ask another salesperson to take care of my needs. If no one else is available look at me, select something you can like about me, and tell yourself that I'm really not so bad after all; then try to get me to like you.

To make me like you don't ask me about my hobbies unless they are directly related to what you are selling. Remember, the big fish on the wall may belong to the last person who occupied the room we are sitting in and my sweatshirt may be a gift from my daughter-in-law, emblazoned with the name of the company she works for. Instead, get me to talk about myself and show an interest in what I say. The best questions to ask for openers are:

What has made you successful?

What has made this, or your, company successful?

Listen to my answers and write notes so you do not forget them. When you take notes, you are:

• Showing me that what I say is important.

• Telling me there is a reason for asking the question.

• Giving yourself something to work with later and making me feel good.

This is the first step toward building a relationship.* If I take notes, I am sending the same message to you.

Asking questions that make sense in the situation and listening without thinking of what you are going to say next is key to making me like you. I will know if you listened and heard what I said.

To earn my trust:

- Give me accurate information.

- Do what you say you will do when you say you will do it.

- Arrive for appointments five minutes early.

- Call to reset an appointment if you are going to be more than five minutes late.

- Do all of this consistently.

Like most people, I translate consistency as dependability and trust those who are dependable. Do not expect to develop a relationship with me instantly, but work at it over time and let me determine when and what kind of relationship it will be.

---

*These questions are politically correct and appropriate in any culture, any country.

If you are pursuing me, do not tell me what you are selling on the first contact or first face-to-face meeting. Prevent me from asking what you are selling by asking me the two questions above and then ask me…

What three things would most improve your…(sales, or profits, or competitive position)? Choose the one that is appropriate. Insist on getting three answers and take notes carefully. The third may not be voiced until after a few minutes of silence, because that is the one I wake up thinking about in the middle of the night. After you've checked your notes, ask me any questions you need to get information that will help you decide how you, or your product, or your team, can help me with the concerns and problems I have revealed. Then tell me you need time to think and ask me for an appointment on a specific day and time two weeks out. Doing this tells me that you do not want to waste your time *or mine*.

I will probably then ask you…

What are you selling, or will what you sell help me?

If your answer is: I don't know but when I come back I will tell you if I can or not and if not I will tell you who I think can; I will give you an appointment. I will also spend time thinking about possible solutions and look forward to discussing them and your ideas with you. I will do this because I will know that you are different. I will think of you as a consultant or counselor.

- You do not have to be selling a complex, high priced product to be a consultant or counselor level sales professional. The salesperson who sold the station wagon was a consultant. The "dress me" salesman is a counselor in women's wear. When they go on vacation, their customers wait for them to return rather than buy from someone else.

- The woman who helped me with the robe and the gentleman that watched me sleep, had two things in common:

  ○ They were sensitive and empathic.

  ○ They were professionals.

Nuff said!

Chapter 11

Customer Care

Customers Come In Two Flavors:
The Arch Fails Without Both Of Them

Look at the Business Arch. Two customer blocks are at the top of the curve, next to the keystone,

where strength is essential: one is new customers; the other is repeat customers.

If they do not remain equally strong, the weight of the business will push them out of place and

the Arch will be in danger of caving in. When it does the business will collapse and

destroy the dreams of everyone in it. All that will be left are unused and unborn ideas.

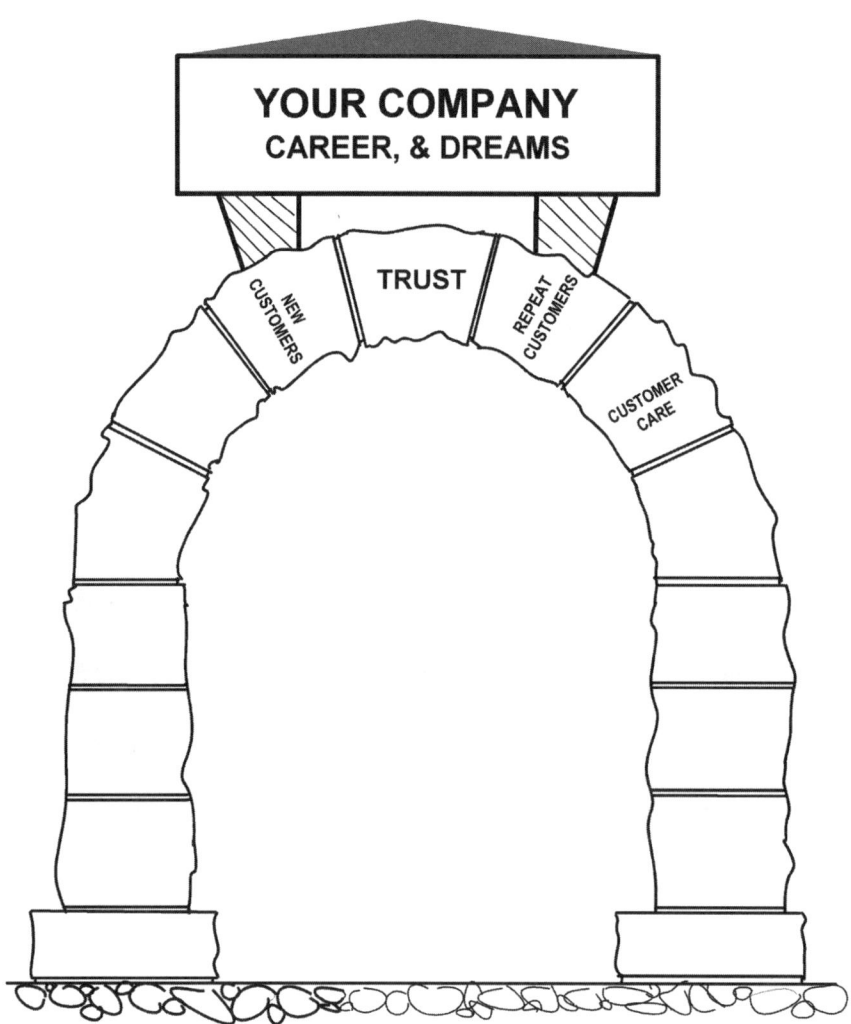

The Business Arch

What Does This Mean?

It means that everyone in the company is responsible for customers. Customers are the only outsiders to the business. They must be attracted and invited into the business: once inside everyone in the business must work to keep them content by maintaining the relationship and satisfying their needs. This requires communication and dialog so that the customer never senses the indifference that leads to loneliness. Feeling indifference accounts for 68 percent of all lost customers. Every person in every function in the Arch is essential to this task. Large or small the most successful companies maintain this Customer Support and Care throughout their existence. In these companies management consistently leads and facilitates the continuing daily care of the customer.

When you and I are part of a small business, we know that our income from the business depends on customers. We get to know them and take care of them because we like them and know our paychecks come from them. When the business grows into a big corporation we often lose sight of this; so do the people in the top floor corner offices.

Rather than be personally involved with customers or you and me, top management often devises policies for us to implement and usually expects us to do it precisely as written. The trouble with this approach is that it leaves us no flexibility and forces us to do things with customers that we know are wrong—wrong because no two customers are alike. We end each day frustrated and angry; we vent this on our most significant other and our children. Then we begin looking for a new place to work. Eventually the top floor people realize that sales are going down and employees are quitting without giving a reason: then the weakened Arch caves in.

If this makes you think that you and I are important you are correct! If you wonder how we can make a difference to customers the answer is:

You and I make a difference to customers with *

What we say and how we say it

What we do and how we do it

each day; not only with customers but with those around us in the workplace. When you and I make a positive difference to them, they in turn make a positive difference to customers they work with. It is that simple. Actually it's easy, particularly when we do it consistently and we must do it consistently.

What we say and how we say it, what we do and how we do it is key to every new customer we bring into the company. The Arch cannot stand without new customers; neither can it stand without customers who give us repeat business. There must be a balance between new and repeat customers both in numbers and the business they give us. If our repeat business comes from only one or two customers, we are in deep yogurt. When our new business depends on landing one big new customer, the yogurt is equally deep. If both of these conditions exist at the same time, the Arch is certain to fail because people in supporting blocks are not doing their jobs. The experience of successful people and businesses shows that consistent Customer Care carried out in small ways results in continuing success. It also shows that it makes these people and companies happy. Examples abound in the pages you have read in this book.

Customer Care is shown in every story throughout the book but not talked about specifically. My point is that we demonstrate the care we will give the customer after the sale, during the Buying, Marketing, and Selling, processes. This is an extremely important item. It is interesting to me that Dan didn't mention it in his four-week sales class, yet I must have done it. If I hadn't I would not have been so successful in landing new customers.

In later years I realized Dan had built the importance of customer care into the selling methodology he taught us. My Dad's methodology had it built in, also. Dan told us to plan our sales calls on a rolling three-week basis so we could tell the new prospect when we would be back. He also pounded into our heads the necessity to call the prospect to confirm (i.e., remind him of) the appointment the week before and always call to set a new time if we were unable to keep the original one. This practice demonstrated that we could be depended upon to deliver what we'd promised when we said we would. This is so simple and yet so profoundly important. It is also the essence of courtesy.

Dan called it time and territory management and we accepted it as such. In doing this consistently we became dependable without realizing it. It became a habit that affected everything I did in life. It strengthened my personal POD in a positive way. Every truly successful person I have worked with has practiced what Dan taught.

Dad did this also but he had one other practice that demonstrated, during the selling process, the Customer Care he would always deliver. It was in his often repeated saying:

"Always think about what is best for the other person."

When you actually do this the other person senses it, relaxes, trusts, and works with you to find the best solution for both of you. You are richer for it.

Customer Care Is Your Personal Responsibility

It is your responsibility every day wherever you are in the company. As cashier or CEO or janitor, the care of the customer is more important than anything else on your schedule. You cannot ignore the question of the person you are checking out because people are lined up behind her. You can be late for that important management meeting if a customer needs help. When you keep the floor clean and dry you are performing Customer Care.

My wife and I were arriving in a large city on different planes from opposite coasts of the United States. She arrived at the hotel in its airport shuttle. After checking her in, the front desk person rang for a bellman to help her with her bags. When a bellman did not arrive quickly he signaled again and a person who was not wearing a bellman's uniform came and picked up the bags. In the elevator he talked with my wife:

"Have you been here before?"

"No. My husband has stayed here several times and will be joining me later today."

"How long are you staying with us?"

"Five days."

He opened the room, walked in, and immediately called the front desk. After a short conversation,

"There is a nicer room with a better view available. It will be more enjoyable for a five-day stay. I'll take you there. The price will be the same as this one."

The room was much nicer. After he had placed her bag on a bench and filled the ice container he refused a tip and told her he would watch for my arrival and bring me to the correct room. A few minutes later a uniformed bellman brought the keys for the new room. When I arrived, the first person took me, and my bags to the room. When the door closed…

"Honey, that bellman doesn't look or act like a bellman. He decided the original room wasn't nice enough and would not accept a tip. He didn't accept a tip from you, either."

"He introduced himself in the elevator. He is the General Manager of this property. I have not met him before. He knew from you or the front desk that I've stayed here before and made his own decisions. I think the room is great."

That hotel chain is one of the world's largest and most successful. It has a Customer Care policy that is outstanding. Everyone is educated, empowered, and funded to keep a customer happy. The bellman can spend a certain amount to make a customer happy without getting permission from a manager. The manager of bellmen can spend a higher amount. The front desk manager has a higher level and the General Manager can do whatever she or he deems necessary. Response to a problem or request is immediate. This is a big corporation policy that is strengthened and renewed with an annual full day, off-site seminar involving the entire staff of each property. This is Customer Care that works. Could this be the reason for the company's consistent success and customer loyalty?

You grow a hotel chain by educating new customers about what you will do for them. You keep them coming back as repeat customers with Customer Care. This keeps both sides of the Arch strong and balanced.

If you are serious about being successful in your work and keeping your company successful you will take or have already taken the time to look throughout this book for all the examples of Customer Care. If not now, then please do it in a few days. It will be worth your time, my friend.

The next story speaks volumes about Customer Care and its ability to build trust and customer loyalty.

My consulting assignment was simple: find out why we are losing existing customers to competition and present your findings at our Club meeting in three months. I asked for and was given a complete list of current and former customers, with permission to make my own arrangements to talk with them. I visited sales offices, interviewed managers and salespeople, and both current and former customers. It was a fabulously interesting task.

The branch managers all wanted some of their customers interviewed; client management told me to go ahead with the result that I finished work on my Club presentation the day I got on the plane. I was scheduled in the number two spot on the first day of Club so no one in the company knew what I was going to say before I walked onto the stage. The CEO and top staff sat in the front row. Unexpectedly, I found myself looking into two spotlights, unable to see my audience and read their reactions…not good, not good.

I began by telling them they were winners, their presence at Club and my experience interviewing them proved that. I then presented a series of graphic slides to show them how and why they were at fault for every lost customer in their territories. I had found no customers who had chosen one of their competitors because of better product capability, quality, dependability, reliability, or price.

Every customer was lost because they had not seen their sales representative or anyone else from the company in three to 12 months, before a competing salesperson called on them. The customer's perception was that the people they had trusted and liked enough to make a major purchase from no longer gave a damn about them and their needs.

Many former customers had discovered they had to call headquarters to order additional equipment. The people in the headquarters order department created the perception that they were doing the customer a favor by taking a $15,000 or $20,000 order because it was a serious disruption of their schedule.

I told them the way to win a sale is to consistently do everything you say you will do, when you say you will, and the way to keep a customer is to make customer service calls on a standing appointment basis. I reminded them that they and the customer had developed a relationship before the order was signed, and the customer did not want it to end when the installation was complete. I used graphics to illustrate all of this. I ended my presentation by again reminding them they were winners who could and would correct these errors in customer service and retention.

I could not see the audience when I said "thank you" and stepped out of the spotlights. There was utter silence as I walked across the stage to the stairs, then there was unbelievable applause. My eyes adjusted to the low light and I realized that everyone was standing except the CEO and his staff. The man who gave me the assignment was standing and clapping hard, so was Amy, in the back of the room, tears streaming down her cheeks as I walked to her side and cried, too.

I learned later that the CEO was angry because I had told his sales stars that they were at fault. The staff members who didn't stand were afraid of his reaction. It was his belief that you should never say anything negative to salespeople, because it would hurt their performance. He was dead wrong.

About four months later the phone rang in my office. It was one of the branch managers who'd listened to me at Club.

"I want you to know that I didn't like what you said at Club. I didn't like being told I was at fault for the lost sales in my branch, but I stood up and clapped with everyone else because I knew I could trust you. Now I need your help and management says they will pay your fee."

"Thank you for telling me that, now how can I help you."

"My team is competing with XXX on a very large installation. We've done the job right, everything you told us at Club, and eliminated all but XXX from consideration. The prospect is giving each of us the opportunity to make one last presentation. XXX is apparently ten percent lower in price than we are. What should we do?"

"Have you offered a discount?"

"No! We are quoting catalog list price. No one in the prospect team has asked for a price break. We only learned about XXX's discount by accident and the prospect doesn't know that we know about it."

"I need a couple of days to think about this; in the meantime, work to have your last and final presentation scheduled after XXX's and do not give any indication that you may be thinking about offering a discount. Don't mention price at all."

We set up a time for our next conversation and I started thinking about their situation. I knew that XXX normally quoted their catalog list price until the last day of a sales situation, when they would, almost invariably, discount the price 15 or 20 percent if the specific sales office was below quota or it was late in XXX's fiscal quarter. I remembered what Dad had said,

"If a man tells you your price is too high, he means he does not see value for his application that justifies your price. If he tells you he can't afford your price, he is telling you he likes your offering and is asking you to show him how to pay for it with his cash flow."

In the first case a discount is needed or you've failed in educating yourself and him. In the second case a payment plan is needed that fits your company's and the prospect's needs. I had learned that when the prospect does not mention price, it isn't a problem in his decision process.

When the branch manager called I was ready.

"Wes, the entire team is listening and we are recording this."

"Keep the entire presentation short, sincere, and speak with confidence and authority. You should practice it live at least twice before you go there. The fact that no one on the prospect team has shown concern about your price tells me it is not a concern. They may bring up price, however, because they will have been given a price 15 to 20 percent lower than list during the presentation by XXX. At the beginning of the presentation you should make the following points in your own words:

During the last months we have shown you the quality of service we provide, by being on time, doing what we promised in the time frame promised, and answering your questions accurately and honestly in a timely manner. We've done this consistently. We will continue to do this consistently for as long as our products meet your needs. Your success will depend on the service we give you. The price we have quoted in our final proposal is no different than we have quoted throughout your decision process. We have done this because by not lowering our price we will be able to afford to continue the level of service we have demonstrated.

Then proceed with the installation work plan, timetable, the people who will implement the installation, and the qualifications of anyone they have not already become acquainted with. Ask for the order and leave with confidence."

There was considerable discussion about this approach and I told them they were probably facing a 15 percent or larger price difference but this approach would overcome that. If it didn't, the prospect would show concern during the presentation, but they should just keep stressing the need to be able to afford good customer service for them.

A few days later the Branch Manager called to thank me and tell me the order was signed without any mention of price. Five or six months later I was a speaker at a meeting of all the client's sales managers. As I was sipping coffee during a break, the Branch Manager who got the order was asked about the sale. He told the group about my involvement.

"Wes told us we would probably be facing a 15 percent price difference. We stressed our service and long-term support and got the order. The installation has gone very well, but I got a real surprise a couple days ago when I went to see the top man and get his input on how we were doing. I always wanted to know if we really had been higher priced so I asked him if that was true. He said 'Yes, their price was 35 percent lower than yours. We trusted your team and we've never been sorry.'…"

To give you perspective, the price was in six figures, no matter whom they bought from.

Did you see the Customer Care in this story?

When and how was it demonstrated and by whom?

What else, what other item or quality is illustrated in this story?

Compare your answers to mine in the next chapter.

Chapter 12

Wes' Last Word

The Keystone In The Arch

Every arch has a keystone. It is the one that is shaped first and placed in position last. The arch is built of blocks put in place from the bottom up, on each side, supported by a scaffold of some sort until the keystone is slipped in place. Then and only then can the scaffold be removed without the arch falling. With the keystone the arch is very strong; without it, the arch cannot stand. You have seen the power of trust throughout the preceding chapters. In the last story you saw trust working in the very practical world of winning and losing customers. What you also saw was the power of Customer Care when administered consistently. What does this tell you?

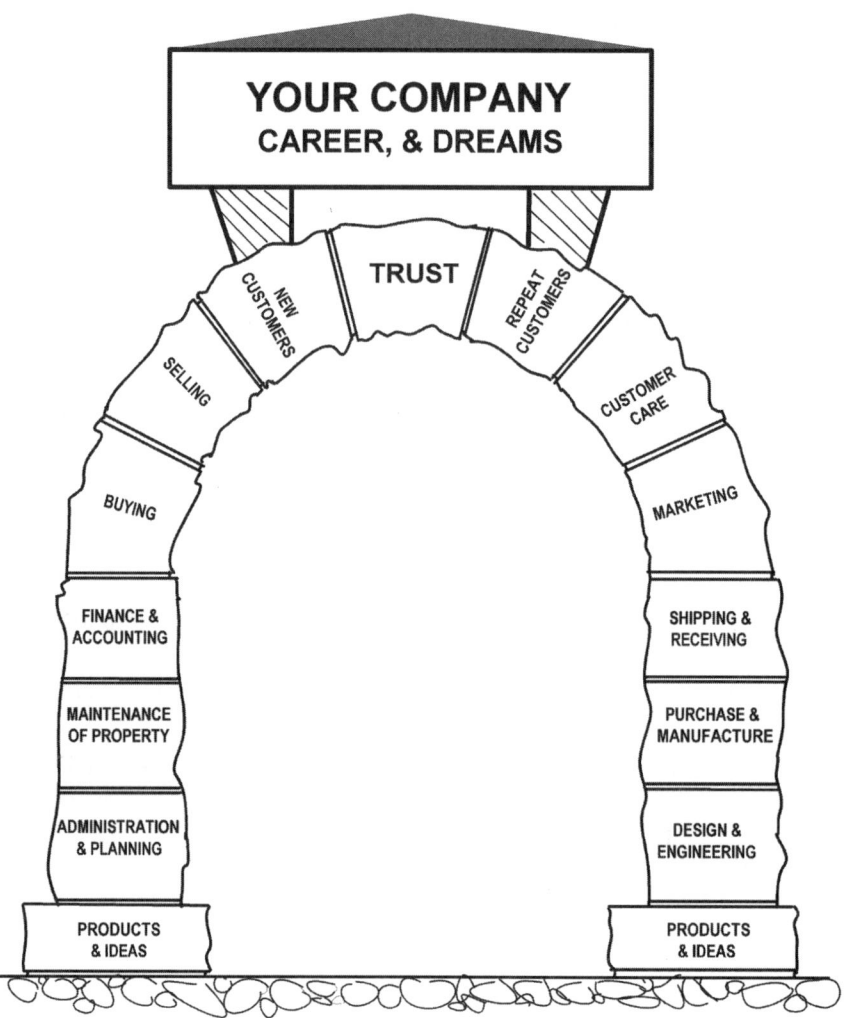

The Business Arch

Look At The Arch

Where is the Customer Care block located in relation to the Trust Keystone?

The Customer Care block is below the Trust Keystone. An Arch is built from the bottom up.

Could the keystone have been installed before the Customer Care block was in place?

Of course not: the Arch cannot be formed without the Customer blocks, which cannot be placed in position without the Customer Care block. Customer Care is essential to maintaining the strength and size of the Repeat Customer block.

Why isn't a Customer Care block supporting the New Customer block?

To answer that question let me ask you another one:

What did you and I learn from the last story about Customer Care?

We learned that Customer Care is essential to creating trust during the Buying process. We saw that it was completely dispersed and integral to the Selling process. If it isn't, a new customer will not be created. That was clearly demonstrated in the story. In practice it was also a part of the marketing that educated the sales team and helped educate the customer.

The other item or quality the story illustrated was trust. Please go back and read the story again.

How many times was trust involved?

In each case, how was it created/earned?

I had to earn the trust of the person that hired me and gave me the assignment. On each interview, I had to earn some level of trust or the person interviewed would not open up to the degree I needed. My presentation to the client's Club would not have taken hold in the minds of my listeners if I had not earned their trust. The sales team had to trust me in order to use my suggestions and risk losing a sale on the basis of price and, of course, the customer had to trust the sales team.

In every case trust was earned through consistency of action, which creates the perception of dependability and honesty. Honesty was evident in my willingness (the CEO said my guts) to show them they were responsible for losing customers. The key here was having factual information presented in a way that forced each of them to look back and remember that they had not called on the customers they had lost. Each customer had to stop trusting them as a first step in the process of buying from someone else. And what about the CEO? He didn't trust his own salespeople. They were good! You've read some of their stories already in this book. Not all of them lost customers; just a small percentage did not know how to maintain relationships without using prime selling hours to do it. Those who were most successful were able to make a difference for their customers by being available when help was needed.

If you are in Marketing, Sales or Customer service/support/care;

Go thou and do likewise.

If you are currently working in any one of the other blocks in the Arch, including one that gives you a top floor corner office, take a hard, thoughtful look at the Arch.

What is the Arch supporting?

What specific blocks do the supporting?

What does that tell you?

The Arch is supporting your life, your career and the source of your happiness, personal satisfaction, dreams of the future, and your income. Your work is integral to all of this because it is a social experience in which you are creative and productive while having fun and enjoyment. You are the company; the organization that provides all of this. You make a difference every day. If the difference you are making is negative, leave the company as quickly as possible. Do this for your own sake and the company's.

How do I make a positive difference?

If I don't or can't for some reason why should I leave?

Take another look at the Arch as a whole: it consists of pieces called blocks. The blocks look solid, don't they? That solid look is only a perception in your mind. In fact, if you look at one of them closely you will find it is made of small particles held together by a substance you can't quite see with your eyes even when using a microscope. I'm describing a concrete or some other stone block.

You are one of the particles in the functional block in which you work. Every one of the people who work in that block with you is another particle. You are held together by a substance, or force you can't see and as long as that remains strong the block remains strong and does its part to hold up the Arch. When it weakens and the block falls apart, one particle/person at a time, the Arch falls in a heap, caving in and destroying everything it has been supporting... that force you can't see is Trust.

Trust Is Like Love

Trust is like love... you must give it before you can receive it.

When you trust those you work with you can make a positive difference to customers directly or through others. When you are in a corner office, the Customer Care policies you develop will be effective because you trust the people who will carry them out with customers. If you don't trust those people you will unconsciously reveal that lack of trust in the way the policies are written; the people involved will distrust you and the policies, carry them out in the way that protects their backsides, and the customers will be unhappy. Your lack of trust creates distrust that weakens multiple blocks in the Arch in addition to the repeat customer block. Look at the Arch:

Where will you be in the heap when it caves in?

New customers join your company, i.e., come into your life and remain as repeat customers when they perceive a positive difference in what you and I say and do as we greet and then serve them. As customers you and I know when the people in a business trust each other and their management; we sense it and feel that we will be trusted, also. After that, real communication takes place between us and the people who are the business. We, and the people that are the business, begin creating a positive perception of a difference in each other's minds; the Arch becomes stronger and all of us have fun.

Yes, trust is the key to success in sales and customer retention. It is the key to success in every business enterprise no matter how big or small. It is the key to happiness in personal relationships.

Trust is also the key to happiness and promotions in a job. If you are not trusted by your work team peers they will make life miserable for you and prevent you from advancing. If your supervisor does not trust you he will never recommend you for promotion. If you do not trust your supervisor or your teammates, you will unconsciously be less attentive to customers, which will weaken the business arch of the company.

If you still have doubts about the importance of trust, count the number of stories in this book where trust is mentioned. In all of them it began with a POD, a Perception Of A Difference that was positive. That perception was created by the first person the customer or other participants saw and talked with; people like you and me. That positive perception was strengthened and maintained by every person in the organization. The tone of voice and sincerity when they said "Good morning" or "May I help you?" or "Come back soon" or "You're a good man, Charlie." The little things make the difference: you make the difference. You are the difference!

Nuff Said!

Thank you for reading this book. I would enjoy knowing your thoughts on its usefulness. I will acknowledge receipt of them whether positive or negative. Remember, I cannot learn and grow if you are not honest with me. I also welcome stories from your experience that support or add new dimensions to the points made in the book. Please indicate if I may use them in other books and publications such as Zimmerman's Zingers and The Perception Of A Difference Quarterly.

—Wes Zimmerman

E-mail *aperceptionofadifference@az.rmci.net*

Fax 480-948-1036

The Four Eternal Laws
Of Sales Success

1. **People Buy From People They Like And Trust!**

2. **Your Present Customer Is Your Best Prospect!**

3. **They Have Never Repealed The Law Of Averages!**

4. **Systematic, Consistent, Effort Assures That You Will Be In The Right Place At The Right Time More Often Than Your Competitor!**

In 1986, I formulated these laws based on my experience and things Dad had said to me. They are applicable to all professional selling situations. If you would like a copy visit:

www.preceptionofdifference.com

Acknowledgments

It has been over five years since I began the effort on this series about The Perception Of A Difference. Five different clients had urged me to write it because of the results the POD had produced in their lives and businesses. What finally forced me to go to work was the receipt of a package containing two thick bound books of blank, lined yellow paper. A note from a wonderful person was clipped to them. It was from Larry Sloan, a man who had benefited from the Perception Of A Difference Program. He had made me his mentor, counselor, and friend. His note simply said: Now, Write! On the first page he had written a foreword for the book. I thank him now and have thanked him in my prayers ever since. He is still a support to me.

The original plan was for a single volume envisioned to be no more than 275 pages in length. From the outset it was to be made up of true stories just as Zimmerman's Zingers had been. I felt this was the best method to pass on the wisdom of the people who had taught me everything and made me a better man in the process. As I wrote, the book became too long to be contained in one volume. I found that as I wrote, stories that long since had been buried in memory resurfaced. I am blessed with the ability to remember conversations quite accurately and relive them. This is how this book came to be. It is the collected wisdom and experience of all those people who made my life so rich.

Some named in the book, who have made multiple incremental differences to me are:

- Amy, the tall girl in the red coat who I liked at once and have loved deeply. We were young, without money, and filled with dreams when we started. We built a life together based on "We" and "Our" instead of "I" and "Mine." It worked; it still works. She is the greatest blessing I have been given.

- Bill, Judy, Paul, and Mark, our children, four of His blessings to us. They are all achievers and all serve others. They are friends to us, and each other; for this I thank God.

- Walt Bailey, my friend, editor, and associate for over 30 years. He is blessed with the ability to study a mass of data, then reach deep inside, select an item, and announce, "If we fix this the rest will take care of itself." He is invariably correct.

- Ralph Sweeney, the man who asked me to join his sales team, then guided, mentored, and supported me to success. I would have paddled a birch bark canoe across hell if he asked me.

- Daniel Merrick, who taught the only formal sales/selling class I ever attended; four wonderful, tough, life changing weeks that I still remember vividly.

- Ms. Bowes, the observant, understanding secretary to Ralph and everyone else in his District Office team. She earned the respect of us all.

- William G. Zimmerman, "Bill" to everyone else, Dad to me. He wasn't perfect but he shaped my life in a way I did not realize until I had been on my own for many years.

I have also been supported in this labor of love by:

- Carol Heitke, my sister, who has proofread these pages more than once.

- Tommy Gillespie, a fine grandson who has used his God given talents in producing the drawings and illustrations in this book.

- Michele DeFilippo, founder of 1106 Design, who offered suggestions while producing the cover and the interior of this book. She is a professional who makes working with her fun and exciting.

- Sharon Tully, sales representative for Central Plains Book Manufacturing. She has educated me about book printing, paper selection, binding, and her company, with enthusiasm and honesty. She is a professional salesperson at the consultant level, and a joy to work with.

- All the others on the WZA team.

You also have a multitude of people in your life who have made and are making a difference to you. Treasure them and make a difference to them. It is worth the effort. It makes your life rich.

Again, thank you for reading this volume. I hope that you read the other volumes because they contain the wisdom of many more people.

—Wesley W. Zimmerman

This Is Volume One In A Series

This is volume one in a series about the Perception Of a Difference (POD), and its power and how it affects everything you and I do. The next volume to be published is in second draft stage at the time of this writing. It will be titled

The Perception Of A Difference (POD)
The Deciding Factor In Your Life

It will tell you how the perception of your difference forms in the mind of another person and what you can do to tilt it toward positive the majority of the time. This knowledge will do more to make your dreams come true than anything else you may learn. You will learn how to apply it to your personal life and relationships, choosing and getting a job, and growing in your chosen career. This volume will also show why managing and leading successfully is absolutely tied to your POD and its effect on decisions others make with and about you.

True stories will provide the insights and wisdom in all the books in the series.

Dad's Sayings

Dad was a gentleman in the true sense of the word, a master salesman, successful business owner, and accurate judge of people. I was never aware that he was teaching me how to be successful in sales and perhaps he wasn't, either, but he did just that. He did it with his sayings, which he repeated many times when I was with him in the normal course of living and working together. They became a part of my POD and the way I have done business. They are mentioned where appropriate in this volume and the others in the series. I list them here because they contain much wisdom that is ageless.

Doing your best was essential to Dad. He told me 100 times or more — *"There is always someone who is better than you but if you always do your best, you will be better than most."*

Other sayings that he repeated countless times are:

- *"Don't be afraid to be different. If you are the same as everyone else you are nothing. Decide who you are and what you are and don't look back."*

- *"Always think about what is best for the other person and don't give him less. If you are selling, think about the other person, not your wallet. If you always sell what is best for the other person, your wallet will be full."*

- *There is some good in everyone so always look for it in the other fellow.*

- *"Don't be half ass about anything."*

- *"If you aren't equipped to do a job, don't take it."*

- *"You will not be a man until you have been fired, quit in a huff, and changed jobs after careful thought."*

- *"When you hate to get out of bed and go to work, it is time to find another job."*

- *"There is nothing more terrible than working at a job you do not enjoy and cannot be proud of."*

- *"Never carry matches. That way you won't be tempted to burn bridges behind you."*

- *"Close doesn't count."*

- *"A miss is as good as a mile."*

- *"Learn something new every day."*

- *"Always be bright and early on the job, but bright is key."*

- *There is no security in a job. Your security and worth is between your ears. Nobody can take that away from you."*

- *"A man charges what he thinks he is worth. If he doesn't charge much he probably isn't worth much."*

- *"Never buy from the low bidder. He has to get well sometime."*

- *"Always be the high bidder or tied for the honor. You may land fewer contracts but you will be in business as long as you want to be."*

- *"If a man tells you your price is too high, he means he does not see value for his application that justifies your price. If he tells you he can't afford your price, he is telling you he likes your offering and is asking you to show him how to pay for it with his cash flow."*

- *"Never put or allow yourself to be put in a compromising position."*

- *"Never dip your pen in the company ink."*

- *"If you cannot walk away, when it's laying on the table in front of you, you are not a man."* This was his way of saying that a man must have the ability to control himself in any situation.

List Of Stories

This is a list of those stories in this volume that have bold face headings.

Some short stories are not included.

The Perception Of A Difference (POD)

The Power In
Buying, Marketing, Selling, Customer Care

Volume One In A Series

Published by
WZA Inc
11060 North 77th Street, Scottsdale, AZ 85260-5564

Illustrations by Tommy Gillespie
Tucson, Arizona

Arch analog drawing by Walter O. Bailey Jr.
Scottsdale, Arizona

Design and layout by 1106 Design
Phoenix, Arizona

Library of Congress Catalog Number pending

ISBN: 0-9760307-0-5

Printed in the United States of America by
Central Plains Book Manufacturing

Market Research (ARC) Edition

The Author

I stood on a hill at midnight under a black sky vivid with stars and a quarter moon. I was 18. I was alone talking out loud with God. I did this several times a week when I came home from my job in a theatre.

Suddenly, I wasn't alone. My perception was that God, this Presence, was real, very real. I sensed that He/It was asking me to serve Him by serving others. I felt intense love, warmth, peace... I said, I will serve you in whatever way you ask. My life changed; silently, permanently.

Five years later...

"Who's the tall girl in the long red coat?"

"I don't know, I've never seen her before."

"Looks like she and her guy are reading a book together."

I wanted to meet her. I did something completely uncharacteristic for me. I walked up behind this couple, stuck my head between their heads, shouldered the man aside, and introduced myself to the lady. Six weeks later she accepted my proposal of marriage.

Eight years later…

I applied for a job as a system support person with a large business equipment company. After taking a battery of tests, I was taken to meet the district manager. He came to the doorway of his office. He asked me two questions. I asked him three. We shook hands and I walked out. He and I talked about that meeting many times in the ensuing years. We agreed that our time face-to-face was less than five minutes; yet, when it ended, I knew I would respect and enjoy working with him and he felt the same way about me. Three weeks later when he called and asked me to join his team as a salesperson, I said yes — even though I'd tried sales once before and did not like it.

These three most important decisions in my life were based on perceptions, positive perceptions that formed in seconds without any conscious thought.

During my sales and marketing career I worked with customers and salespeople all over the world, helping them to succeed in making their dreams come true while working with them as their peer, manager, leader, consultant, and mentor. I have been successful in manufacturing and sales management, professional sales, marketing, and business ownership. I also became a certified Lay Pulpit Supply for the Evangelical Lutheran Church in America; and in that capacity, I filled in for sick pastors on many occasions.

At age 51 I became a business consultant. I used my experience and insight to help client companies and their employees to reach their goals. It was then that I realized I had been using the *Perception of a Difference* most of my life and that sharing its power had enabled me to help hundreds of others to reach their personal goals. Learning about and using the *Perception of a Difference* brought the people in 95 companies personal satisfaction and happiness and enabled them to move their companies to success and stability.

I've been writing all my life and developed a style that communicates with the reader. The CEO of a large corporation said,

"Wes, you write the way you talk."

It has served me well in helping others.

Zimmerman's Zingers© was originally aimed at salespeople in Honeywell Information Systems. They were fun to read and filled with useful ideas; management at all levels asked for them. *Zimmerman's Zingers*© reached every level of the company worldwide. The *Zingers* continued as a subscription publication for my consulting clients and was joined by *The Perception Of A Difference Quarterly (PDQ).*© Both were published for several years. I have also written many articles for various trade publications. I have learned a great deal from starting and operating two service businesses and working with the people in client businesses ranging in size from three to 175,000 team members.

I realize now, that as a result of that experience on the hill that night, every job and position I've held in life has been one in which I was used to help others. I, and the tall girl in the long red coat have had fun for 54 years. Becoming a professional salesperson financed the fun and all the family responsibilities that resulted. I have had a rich, full life, filled with love, respect, and satisfaction because of the power of perceptions and the ability to create *a perception of a difference* and, *make* a positive difference.